My America
Wake Up
Be Proud

By Eric F. Sidler
© 2013

My America Wake Up Be Proud

My America Wake Up Be Proud

By Eric F. Sidler ....© 2013

Published by ....http://www.lulu.com

ISBN 978-1-304-34878-4

Contact the author:

esidler@tampabay.rr.com

My America Wake Up Be Proud

My America Wake Up Be Proud

Table of Contents

My America Wake Up Be Proud...3
Table of Contents..5
Acknowledgements 7
Introduction 9
Chapter 1..12
  A Dream Comes True 12
Chapter 2..18
  My Background..18
Chapter 3..22
  My Jobs 22
Chapter 4..39
  My Company..39
Chapter 5..53
  Banking and Beyond 53
Chapter 6..70
  The Environment and Beyond 70
Chapter 7..75
  Religion and Beyond...75
Chapter 8..85
  Health, Addictions and Beyond 85
Chapter 9..100
  My Beautiful America..100
Chapter 10...112
  About Marriage 112
  Chapter 11 115
Chapter 12...122
Politics and Beyond 122
  Dark Forces 115

My America Wake Up Be Proud

Acknowledgements

Editorial
& Insights from
Marilyn Ann
Ellsworth

Content
Contributions
From
Bill Lane
Robert Friedman

Cover Design
By
Glenna Blomquist
&
George Sawyer

My America Wake Up Be Proud

Introduction

"My America Wake Up Be Proud." Those who take this title literally, are certainly right. Those who hear a subtle admonishment are equally correct.

In a suspenseful panorama of personal experiences, good as well as bad, the author peppers his analytical and critical observations with humor and often biting comments.

His colorful picture of America is honed by his vast international experience, born and raised in the model country of Switzerland for twenty-two years.

He served in the U.S. Army to become a naturalized citizen. Later he traveled the whole world on behalf of *The Wall Street Journal* for fourteen years headquartered at their London Office.

After establishing his own business in Germany with a subsidiary in Paris, France and a holding in Geneva, Switzerland, he studied for thirty years corporate and political successes and failures in all major countries and drew his own conclusions which he applies with surprising insights to the United States.

Such an in-depth analysis of the U.S. can only be drawn by a totally independent spirit free of peer pressure and fully ignoring political correctness.

His all encompassing observations about politics, finance, religion, the environment, and marriage give ample thought for substantial and tolerant debate. His travelogue throughout the U.S. rounds up his positive attitude for his beloved America.

With his international background he is uniquely qualified to analyze, compare and draw his own, often, challenging conclusions.
In a quarter page review of Sidler's book about Germany, The Editor in Chief of the leading business and financial daily, *The Handelsblatt*, commented in the introduction: "This is a passionate declaration of affection from a prominent guest-worker to Germany. Eric F. Sidler, who established the first international Financial Communications Company in Frankfurt, doesn't mince words in his critical evaluation. If it weren't critical and

sometimes biting, the author, known for his unfearing language, would disappoint us."

Some of these same qualities are inherent in this book "My America Wake Up Be Proud." It is a pleasurable, yet, challenging read with many ideas, recommendations and admonishments, well worth thinking about.

Chapter 1

A Dream Comes True

There she towered, the Statue of Liberty, the symbol of freedom, the gift from the French. The luxury liner, The SS United States, listed slightly portside with so many fellow travelers wanting to catch a glimpse of this impressive Lady.

It was 1954, my dream had come true. I was on my way to immigrate to the USA. It was an unusual development for I had been studying law at the University in Zurich, Switzerland, when my father found out that I was hardly attending courses, chasing girls, drinking beer and playing cards instead. He was no longer prepared to pay for my escapades. I had flunked third grade after I made it quite clear that I disapproved of the incompetence of the teacher. Later, in a school for difficult boys of well-off parents, I was taught some manners and succeeded in advancing to the second best in class.

My father, a tolerant, highly successful publisher and national political figure, enquired what I wanted to do with my life. My answer was terse: "I want to become a Hollywood actor." My idols at that time in my life were stars such as Humphrey Bogart,

James Cagney, Gary Cooper and Jimmy Stewart. My father took me to lunch to meet one of the most successful Swiss stars, Heinrich Gretler, who had a leading role in one of the few internationally successful Swiss movies, Heidi, the first movie in Technicolor. He was supposed to convince me that my intentions weren't well thought out. Of course, he achieved the opposite, because I felt he was just an old nay-sayer.

In addition, I well remembered the generosity and open kindness of the American soldiers that came to Switzerland for relaxation after the Second World War. They gave me chocolate, chewing gum, nylon stockings and even condoms which I sold to grown-ups to the great annoyance of my father. After all, I had been only around 15.

My wish was discussed extensively in the family. My mother was not in favor at all. My father reviewed his options for he had to find an American citizen to sponsor me, who had to guarantee ten thousand U.S. dollars security for me. In 1954 this was a great deal of money, around a hundred thousand U.S. dollars in today's dollars. Fortunately, with his business connections, he found

14

a sponsor and I was ready to immigrate. He bought a one way ticket, business class, on The SS United States and handed me four hundred dollars. He intoned in a friendly voice: "Only come back if you can pay for the return trip yourself."

The voyage was a grand experience, excellent food and drinks, cinema and dancing, all the comfort of a luxurious life. I joined a group of young Americans and soon realized that my school English, embellished by movie dialogue learned from dubbed films, was not enough to converse fluently with my new found friends. One attractive young student invited me to visit her in upstate New York to meet with her parents. I happily accepted, hoping for an enjoyable affair. I wasn't aware that at that time in the U.S., a decent girl wanted to remain a virgin until marriage; quite a disappointment for a more liberal minded Swiss. I soon found out that the moral standards, at least on the surface, were very strict. Playboy was still banned in many states and the illegitimacy rate was extremely low. Hollywood had a strict moral code and movies had no lewd scenes or open sex.

I had great expectations when arriving in New York having seen all the glitter and beauty of the country in films. The first letdown was the conditions of the New York docks. They were dilapidated and I spotted some rats. First and Second Avenue were dirty, run down, poor districts with third rate housing, cheap shops and grimy restaurants. Garbage was strewn all over the streets. It was pure filth for someone coming from prim and proper Switzerland. Matters improved somewhat after Lexington and Madison Avenue and finally I enjoyed upscale Fifth Avenue.

The cab driver brought me to the Sheraton Hotel where my father had reserved a room since the manager was a native Swiss. A single room was nineteen dollars and fifty cents plus tax. Having only four hundred dollars and no job, I asked the manager if he could recommend a place I could afford. He suggested the Young Men's Christian Association, better known as the YMCA at Twenty Third Street.

Having lived in Zurich, Switzerland in a beautiful, large house overlooking a lake, sleeping in a comfortable, nice bedroom, the YMCA, seemed at that time, a dirty, rundown shelter for the unsuccessful.

Everybody warned me not to go out at night alone since it wasn't safe. Picturesque Central Park was a dangerous place at night. That was in the fifties when New York ranked high in the world league of crime. In contrast, today, New York is safer than Zurich, Switzerland.

The reason for Zurich's downward spiral is uncontrolled immigration. The average Swiss do not want to work in hotels or restaurants, perform cleaning jobs or work in lower level manual tasks. After WWII the Swiss took in guest-workers from Italy who caused little or no problems. Perhaps they added louder and happier voices, more gesticulation when talking and exuding a zest for life; quite in contrast to the often somber, reserved German Swiss. But the Italians returned to their homeland when their economy started to boom. The Swiss then turned to the Turks to get much needed guest-workers. The result was an increase in petty crimes and overall less safety in the major cities. But life was still tolerable.

Everything deteriorated when the Turks left as their economy started to grow. The Swiss then turned to other nations where violent crime is part of the national pastime. Crime fears have increased by around fifty percent in the past three years according to a recent survey, and concerns about being mugged or robbed are up by twenty percent.

As a native Swiss having lived twenty two years in Switzerland, in Lucerne as a boy and later in Zurich, I have witnessed the decline in safety. Gone are the days of unlocked cars, apartments and houses. There also is open drug dealing and use around major cities. In stark contrast you can now safely wander in Central Park in the evening and enjoy the splendor of New York by night. That's progress!

New York bit the bullet with tough law enforcement and support from the mayors succeeded in dramatically reducing the crime rate. Meanwhile Zurich went in the opposite direction with lax laws and open tolerance of drug use, following the example of Amsterdam. The results speak for themselves as to which is the better policy.

Chapter 2

My Background

In school, college and at the Zürich University my favorite disciplines were languages, mathematics, economy, history and philosophy. My fantasy about the United States was mainly nourished by the many movies I enjoyed and by the romantic wild-west stories told by my favorite authors Zane Grey and the German author Karl May.

Among the philosophers, I was a fan of French writer Blaise Pascal remembering his statement: "Human beings must be known to be loved. Devine beings must be loved to be known." Another good quote is: "Men never do evil so completely and cheerfully as when they do it from religious conviction."

I smiled at Schopenhauer with his infamous remark about women: "It is only man whose intellect is clouded by his sexual impulse that could give the name of the fair sex to that under-sized, narrow-shouldered, broad hipped and short-legged race; for the whole beauty of sex is bound up in this

19

impulse." At that time women were indeed short-legged in stark contrast to today's gracious, long and slim-legged women in The States. But some of his other thoughts are worth reading: "Great men are like eagles and build their nest on some lofty solitude. Wealth is like sea-water, the more you drink, the thirstier you get; and the same is true of fame." For another smile: "In our monogamous part of the world, to marry means to halve one's rights and double one's duties." Without doubt, one of his best observations is: "All truth passes through three stages. First it is ridiculed. Second, it is violently opposed. Third, it is accepted as self-evident."

I didn't care much for Emanuel Kant with his categorical imperative, but I certainly admired Bertrand Russell, who said: "The trouble with the world is that the stupid are cocksure and the intelligent are full of doubt. One should respect public opinion insofar as is necessary to avoid starvation and keep out of prison, but anything that goes beyond is voluntary submission to an unnecessary tyranny." That goes as well today for peer pressure and political correctness! My father's best comment was: "Stupidity is a gift of God but one shouldn't misuse it."

I was an early admirer of Sir Winston Churchill who is the only human being I waited for in line to see when he came to the Swiss capital of Berne for a visit. I well remember some of his more profound statements that should be read out loud by most politicians today in Washington: "Socialism is a philosophy of failure, the creed of ignorance, and the gospel of envy: its inherent virtue is the sharing of misery." So much for class warfare with the battle cry "soak the rich!"

Looking at some leaders on the left and right in Washington today, I am reminded of his remark: "A fanatic is one who can't change his mind and won't change the subject."

As to Foggy Bottom, the derogatory name for the State Department, the claim that a video was responsible for the attacks in Benghazi, Churchill's comment comes to mind: "A lie gets halfway around the world before the truth has a chance to get its pants on."

With the ultra right being driven by greed and the ultra left by envy, Churchill's comment: "The inherent vice of capitalism is the unequal sharing of blessings; the inherent virtue of socialism is the equal sharing of miseries," seems appropriate.

And finally, about the Americans he barked: "You can always count on the Americans to do the right things after they've tried everything else." We shall see if Washington sees the light eventually, remembering his statement: "If you have thousands of regulations you destroy all respect for the law." The approval rating of Congress today, being below ten percent bears ample testimony to these pearls of wisdom.

Many pundits and leaders of industry finance and politics shaped my mind and gave me the courage to ignore political correctness, as well as peer pressure.

Chapter 3

My Jobs

In Zurich, in the early fifties, I worked during the summer vacation at an advertising agency which was run by a friend of my father, which was probably the reason I got the opportunity.

As a Swiss, I also had to serve in the Swiss Army for four months. These were without doubt the toughest months of my entire life. At that time, the Swiss Army was merciless with softies and the training could be downright cruel. When on maneuver in the snowy Swiss Alps we got soaking wet, but were not allowed to dry our uniform during the night. It had to be neatly folded at the bottom of the bunk. Colds and pneumonia were not uncommon results of this idiotic practice.

The food was unbearable and once a month we had to eat canned food with the cans dating back to the Second World War. Even though they were often full of worms, the sergeant made sure we finished the meal.

Every physically fit Swiss man has to serve in the Armed Forces. After this duty, he is required to take care of his rifle at home to be ready for any emergency.

In sharp contrast, I joined the US Army in order to become a US citizen after an honorable discharge. I couldn't believe the luxury, the different uniforms and the excellent boots and shoes we were issued. When I was asked in the chow line if I wanted pie-a-la-mode for dessert, I thought the server was making fun. Those two years were without doubt a true highlight of my life.

That was also the time when I was confronted with racism. My unit had ninety percent black soldiers mostly from Brooklyn, and only a handful of whites. When going out with my buddies, I always chose the blacks as my companions. They were definitely more fun. However, after a couple of weeks their top honcho told me I couldn't join them anymore because some of his friends didn't like whities. Well, as a native Swiss, I was totally unaware of color and black, yellow or brown meant nothing to me. I admired men like Louis Armstrong, Fats Waller, Earl "Fatha" Hines and Gandhi.

This incident reminds me of when I visited my family after being discharged. I traveled in my uniform for I was proud to be an American. However, my mother disapproved and made me change into civilian clothes with the comment that Americans were narrow minded the way they treated their black citizens. A few days later we went together by train to Zurich. She refused to enter one particular carriage because she said it was full of dirty and noisy Italian guest-workers. Well, so much for racism. I believe, in all of us, there is some latent prejudice, even if we do not want to acknowledge it.

On a boat to Panama I volunteered, even though other soldiers warned me never to volunteer. The sergeant was looking for five soldiers with personnel experience. He informed us that we would be helping the civilian Job Analysts after the Administration had decided to reevaluate all jobs trying to save money.

The sergeant warned me that my English wasn't good enough, but he said it was worth a try. Thanks to his choice, I was active as a Job Analyst after some solid training by an older woman who theoretically became my boss. I got my own car and interviewed any and all jobs from bakery mechanics to geologists. After writing the job description, I had to grade the job in accordance with the given standards and my boss checked my work and made necessary improvements. It was a God given opportunity to learn the fine points of the English language and all the special words in each profession. However, to downgrade individuals that had performed the same job for many years was a sad reminder of the often unjustified actions, when governments decide to save money.

After my discharge I was required to take an oath on the Bible to become an American citizen. When I refused, because at that time I was an atheist, the captain made it quite clear that if I continued to refuse I couldn't get my citizenship. Well, my choice was clear. I then nearly decided to stay in Panama as a civilian joining the Civil Service as a junior Job Analyst.

My first job after arriving in the U.S. was as a busboy at the Roosevelt Hotel, cleaning tables while Guy Lombardo was playing there. I was soon promoted to the reservation department and later to the front desk. That's when I decided the hotel business was not for me especially in view of the low pay scale. I joined an advertising agency supply company as a sales trainee where my kind boss, borne in Alsace Lorraine, France, enjoyed speaking French with me. He encouraged me to complete enough time in the Army to become an American to get ahead in business.

After the Army I went to colorful San Francisco traveling by train from New York. It was a great lesson in the broad spectrum of American life. I stopped in St.Louis to visit Anheuser Busch where the wife of one of the owners was from Lucerne. They offered me a job merchandising beer, but I didn't think that was my future. I also visited a local church where they were still using snake rites. I was probably the only white person having dared to enter.
I traveled to L.A. to visit a top power company in Riverside that was looking for a job analyst to set up a grading system. I was tempted, but decided

Riverside was not what I was looking for to settle into.

It was in San Francisco where I hit the jackpot. *The Wall Street Journal* was advertising for a trainee. Remembering my father's successful career in the newspaper business, I applied for the job. I was hired at one of the most admired and at that time extremely profitable organizations on the planet.

My new boss took me out to dinner and suggested that we visit a night club afterwards. He had heard that they featured a decent program. The star of the show was a hypnotist and my boss asked me to go on stage as a volunteer. I pointed out that I learned how to hypnotize when I was around sixteen. I explained I had succeeded in putting a much younger boy into a trance, but wasn't able to wake him up. He recovered; however, this was my first and last attempt at this art.

Since that experience, no hypnotist was able to put me into a trance and I suggested to my boss that he should go on stage instead. The hypnotist asked him if he had some friends or acquaintances abroad and my boss told him about his uncle in Australia. After he put him in a trance, he asked him if he saw his uncle and he should tell us what he was doing. He answered: "He is grilling shrimp, preparing a rice salad and drinking Heineken beer." The hypnotist woke him up and asked him to call his uncle. He had to get the phone number by calling his wife first and came out on stage later. He called his uncle, who confirmed every thing he had seen in his trance.

This spontaneous happening confirmed my firm belief that all thoughts are miniscule electric currents that travel through the universe and can be received under certain circumstances. It strengthened my conviction that all knowledge is in the universe and that humans have never discovered anything except having profited from accessing available resources. It explains how Leonardo da Vinci, Einstein and other geniuses were and are able to envision developments in the distant future.

After only a few weeks in San Francisco, which I immensely enjoyed, the boss in New York, who had read my application, decided my knowledge of languages and my Swiss background were ideal to complement the business side of their one man editorial office in London. Once there, my job was

29

to sell *The Wall Street Journal* to Europeans and introduce other Dow Jones Services. *The Wall Street Journal* as well as its sister publication *Barron's* and the company's Broad Tape controlled much of the news emanating from powerful Wall Street at that time, with little or no competition.

It was a tremendous opportunity for a 25 year old business greenhorn. The name *Wall Street Journal* had immense magic at that time. The paper had less than one hundred thousand circulation and only sixteen pages per day, which slowly crept up to twenty four. There was no question in my mind but that such a prestigious opportunity for an inexperienced young man, offered by such a fine corporation, could only happen in America. I was given a yearly budget and didn't even have to account for my expenditures.

The name *Wall Street Journal* opened most doors of top executives in the United Kingdom, Germany, France, Italy, Switzerland, the Scandinavian Countries, Spain and Portugal to name some of the major markets for Dow Jones products. During my thirteen years with this sterling company which ranked in the fifties among the top most profitable corporations in the U.S., I advanced to European Manager and in the mid sixties I was promoted to International Director covering the entire industrialized world except the U.S., Canada and the Caribbean. What a golden opportunity to get to know the business and financial leaders of these countries, not as a tourist but as a well paid businessman! I built up a global network of local representatives who were working on commission and the revenue from international clients grew steadily.

The Germans were particularly interested in a closer dialogue with the Americans after their industries slowly started to regain recognition throughout the world, and I convinced New York to open an office in Frankfurt which later became the seat of my own company.

My years with *The Wall Street Journal* provided me with a deep insight as to what made businesses successful in the United Kingdom, Sweden, Switzerland, Germany, Italy, Hong Kong, Japan or Australia: all countries I visited regularly. My extensive travels also had some pitfalls. In Sri Lanka, then Ceylon, I was invited by the Finance

Minister for lunch, and during our conversation I suggested they should package the tea in their country rather than shipping it in bulk to the United States and Britain. This made economic sense to me creating jobs in their country. The idea made the front page in *The Ceylonese Times*. However, my boss was furious. The President of the leading American tea company complained to the President of Dow Jones and I was told to talk only about the virtues of Dow Jones without giving economic advice. I had to get more familiar with corporate culture!

I was delighted to learn that a member of the editorial staff also got into deep waters when a story about GM, one of the biggest advertisers, annoyed its President. He cancelled all advertising in *The Wall Street Journal*, a big blow to the company. Luckily, *The New York Times* picked up the story and castigated GM for its action. The President of GM visited New York after this story broke and settled the matter in favor of Dow Jones. There was no legal battle and all advertising was resumed. I cannot imagine anything like this happening today with *The New York Times* having become a political mouthpiece for one party only.

The President of Dow Jones, Barney Kilgore, was a brilliant, quiet genius, not an eagle on some lofty solitude, but a down to earth manager. He regularly visited every floor in the small building on Broad Street talking with staff members and getting familiar with their daily tasks rather than taking the elevator and making decisions in a vacuum at the top. His management philosophy was dubbed by experts: "Managing by walking around." This successful management style is practiced by many Owners and Partners in many small and medium sized companies. He also developed the highly successful Front Page, two columns, *"What's News,"* feature which has been copied by most business newspapers throughout the world.

The Editor in Chief, William H. Grimes wrote in 1951: "On our editorial page we make no pretence of walking down the middle of the road. Our comments and interpretations are made from a definite point of view. We believe in the individual, in his wisdom and his decency. We oppose all infringements on individual rights, whether they stem from an attempt by a private monopoly, labor union monopoly or from an overgrowing government. People will say we are conservative or reactionary. We are not much interested in labels but if we were to choose one, we would say we are radical. Just as radical as the Christian doctrine." Some of today's pundits should read this statement slowly to begin to understand what is wrong today in many political centers of the world.

If he had lived to witness the intrusion of Washington in our daily lives, his idea of overgrowing government would surely have become a beacon on the Hill.

The Wall Street Journal promotion department regularly conducted ad readership studies when the paper had less than one hundred thousand circulation and only sixteen to twenty pages per day. The results were pretty constant with a full page, depending of course on its content, garnering an average readership of between forty and fifty percent. One day it dropped dramatically and no one knew the answer except an employee in the retail department. He pointed out that it was a Jewish holiday. This proved the vast positive influence the Jewish business community had in the financial district. The highest noted score of any full page was an advertisement featuring a scantily clad Marilyn Monroe type woman promoting a well known magazine. The ad got over ninety percent noted score which says a lot about *The Wall Street Journal* male readership at that time.

When I tried to convince the New York Management of the viability of a European Edition, I was looking for a partner and had a meeting with media mogul Rupert Murdoch, who made the caustic remark: "I doubt if the conservative, mid-western management of *the Journal* would be willing to negotiate with me." Well, after the family owners of Dow Jones made some poor management changes with profits dropping dramatically, Murdoch finally succeeded in negotiating and buying this once great company which still has a flagship, great editorial product, *The Wall Street Journal*.

I also tried to interest Lord Thomson of Fleet, the Canadian borne newspaper tycoon, who controlled *The London Times* and the successful *Sunday Times*. He didn't think bringing the power of *The Journal* to Europe, was a good idea. The New York management had big plans at that time to make *The*

Journal a national newspaper with printing centers in several locations: Europe ranked low on their list of priorities. This was evident when I arranged some meetings for the President, Barney Kilgore, during his first visit to Europe.

After thirteen years headquartered and living in London, traveling up to eight months a year, I wanted a change. Returning to New York was an excellent option, but I decided to leave the company, which in retrospect was not necessarily the smartest choice.

London society and its vibrant night life with the fabulous discotheques of the sixties was a great diversion from the hectic pace of my business life. I met some of the top entertainment stars together with my beautiful and kind Swedish wife: among them were Judy Garland, Steve McQueen and the suave Roger Moore. Jackie Collins, sister of the Dynasty Star, Joan Collins stayed at my house while recuperating from a small operation. She became a well known novelist and both my wife and I thought very highly of her.

For me the typical British businessman was a very kind, somewhat reserved individual, usually with a great sense of humor and a strong determination to succeed at what he was doing. This was especially true at the higher echelons on Fleet Street, at top companies and banks. Most were self assured, but rarely arrogant, which could not be said of some of their German counterparts.

The understatement of some British executives was humorously demonstrated by Sir Cyril Kleinwort, the chairman of Kleinwort and Benson, one of the most prestigious merchant banks of its time, by riding his bicycle to the office every morning. When it rained he wore a tattered, old raincoat. Once, when he invited me to lunch at the executive suite, a butler brought in the entire meal. When he left, the door was locked and the Chairman served his guests. This was privacy in the extreme. Meanwhile, in today's U.S.A., the top man of the CIA corresponds with his paramour using the totally insecure email. Obviously, the male sex drive obfuscates simplest truths.

The entire atmosphere in Central London in the sixties was one of elegance and dignity, an ideal place to enjoy a few years of your life. There were some early signs, however, of trouble developing with uncontrolled immigration. One of the leading politicians, Enoch Powell, was trying to warn his countrymen of the dire consequences of these policies. He became a hate figure of the ultra left. The idea of a multicultural society took hold in Europe, spearheaded by the Dutch, who now, after experiencing its pitfalls dropped this noble undertaking, realizing that some human beings are anything but noble.

It can be argued that Switzerland is a highly successful multicultural society with the French, German and Italian Swiss, forgetting that their Christian roots are identical, only the language and the way of life differs. However, today with over twenty five percent of the population being non-Swiss, there is a great amount of resistance to this trend. The same is true in Canada and in the U.S.A. The Dutch have now made a complete about- face recognizing that immigrants must integrate, speak Dutch and accept the Dutch way of life. The U.S.A. will, hopefully, eventually follow this new trend with the demand that an American must speak English to succeed. After all, the early immigrants, including me, accepted that English was the country's legal language. Why "Dial 2 for Spanish?" No one offered me "Dial 2 for German."

Our experience with the British National Health system was less reassuring. My wife developed a severe toothache, shortly after we arrived in London in 1957 and we selected a dentist near our home from the directory. He wanted to pull five teeth. My wife was horrified and came home rather upset. I told my highly efficient assistant at the office what happened. After checking the name of the dentist she informed us that he was working on National Health where he was getting one pound for pulling a tooth and only ten shillings for filling it. In addition, after pulling some teeth he could sell bridges, etc. and earn good money. She strongly recommended visiting an accredited private dentist. The one we selected found only two teeth needing attention. An isolated case? Hardly!

In retrospect my thirteen years at *The Wall Street Journal* formed and strengthened my beliefs: the substance and the economic understanding that guided me well thru the rest of my life.

Chapter 4

My Company

Dow Jones was more than generous when I left, letting me take-over their German office in the financial capital of Frankfurt and being able to continue to represent *The Wall Street Journal* on commission in this booming market. This prestigious base made it possible to get other top business publications such as the leading Japanese business newspaper, *The Nihon Kaizai Shimbun* and *Forbes*.

The positive flow of revenue gave me the opportunity to establish a new company in partnership with the foremost British company in financial communications to bring the Anglo-Saxon public relations and advertising know-how to Germany. Within only a few years we succeeded in advising fifteen of the top twenty German Banks on how to present themselves in the major capital markets of the Western World. At the same time, we expanded our client base with leading U.S. financial institutions tapping our European know-how.

The client list included Deutsche Bank, the leading German financial institution, for which we organized their first press conference in London. It was no easy task to change their way of dealing with the press because the chairman was also the only official spokesman and other board members did not speak to the press at that time. Daimler Benz, BMW, Volkswagen, Bayer, Siemens and Veba rounded out our prestigious German client list. Merrill Lynch and American Express were some of the top addresses from the U.S.; from Switzerland we serviced the noble private bank, Bank Julius Baer and from the U.K., Barclays Bank and Midland Bank. Our services included annual reports, press conferences, crisis management, television training, speech writing, advertising, product development and organizing major receptions with top speakers such as Central Bankers, Henry Kissinger and other luminaries.

The leading German quality newspaper, *The Frankfurter Allgemeine Zeitung*, referred to our company as the leading financial communication and financial advertising company on the Continent at that time.

For my personal development it was an ideal opportunity to get to know the top echelon of German Industry and Finance and to absorb their business acumen and management ability. I began to understand the immense success of Germany and can sympathies with today's reaction of average Germans that are tired of financing some of Europe's laggards. Their Chancellor, Angela Merkel, is critically referred to as "Mother Theresa of Europe" by some.

In my book about Germany, <u>Mein geliebtes Deutschland</u>, nearly a best seller, with excellent reviews by the foremost business newspaper, *The Handelsblatt*, and the quality daily, *The Frankfurter Allgemeine Zeitung*, I went into details about the German work ethic, their diligence and hard work. With around forty German staff at our Frankfurt office my admiration of their daily performance grew every day. However, I was critical of the government's unfettered immigration policies, the high taxation, the explosion of the crime rate and the overly generous National Health system.

My personal experience with the German health system rivaled our disappointment in London. After getting hit by a car from the back I developed serious pain and decided to visit the doctor next door. The waiting room was full of Turkish guest-workers on that Monday morning. I was treated first, being on private insurance and I asked the doctor about all these workers in the waiting room. He explained that every one of them was going to complain about some pain he couldn't check out to get a few days off on full pay, sick leave, to visit their families in Turkey, a pretty costly affair for the German taxpayer.

Another development disappointed me. The high taxation started to squeeze small and medium sized businesses, and cheating became a routine. Many tradesmen when giving a cost estimate asked: "Cash or Check?" The difference was between ten and fifteen percent. In Italy and France tax evasion became even more widespread stemming from a deep aversion to the central government. The result was the introduction of a high sales tax, over twenty percent to collect the needed revenue. The average Italian also became totally fed up with the antics of his central government and its reckless spending.

Even the Germans are slowly developing a disdain for its encroaching central government in Bonn. With the approval rating of the U.S. Congress being below ten percent, the only question is, when will the average U.S. citizen follow his European counterparts? Obviously, some of the shrewd and lazy have already learned how to cheat their government. A doctor having worked for the Social Security Administration to check out citizens on Social Disability pointed out to me, that with enough staff the number could be cut by around fifty percent. His estimate may be high but it explains what is dramatically wrong with these programs.

With the top German car companies on our client list, I learned first hand how different types of ownership affect success.

Volkswagen, at that time, was government owned. It had only one product, the Beetle, a top seller, incorporating the best of German engineering, having been developed by the genius Ferdinand Porsche. Everybody at Volkswagen was extremely polite and worked with German efficiency, but the company made little or no profit. They invested millions in new designs which never hit the market.

It was a typical, government owned behemoth with a gigantic bureaucratic staff shuffling research papers and trying to be efficient. After it was sold and managed by a relative of Ferdinand Porsche it became a highly profitable and technically superior company. Their modern factory in the center of Dresden bears ample testimony of what private ownership can accomplish. It attracts thousands of visitors who marvel at the open assembly line where mechanics work in white uniforms with gloves. It is glass enclosed and absolutely spotless.

BMW was another government owned car company. The last model under government control was a complete flop and the company was sold off to a tough private investor who brought one of his lawyers in to shape up the management, design and production staff. The rest is history, with the "ultimate driving machine" ranking today among the top cars in the world.

In the sixties, Daimler Benz was in private hands, majority owned by the Deutsche Bank which ruled with its typical dictatorial style. Journalists were barely tolerated and clients had to wait in line over a year to get one of their superb, tractor like, passenger cars. Only a few were sold in the US via a sales genius dealer in New York. Pressure mounted to speed up delivery and modernize design and today with Italian design help and less dependence on the Deutsche Bank it has become an attractive, technically superior company. When its shares were introduced at the New York stock exchange, the American analysts realized and criticized the clever accounting maneuvers to minimize the heavy taxation in Germany. Of course, nobody, not even the German tax authority, dared to criticize the Deutsche Bank's monopoly type behavior, as the owner.

Finally, Porsche was a family owned, small company producing only a couple of cars a day. Every engine had the signature of the responsible technician engraved and German housewives were sewing the convertible tops. My first model with sixty horsepower still had many parts from the Volkswagen. Around forty Porsches later, including those for my wife, I can only claim with prejudice, that the Turbo S is one of the super sport cars of the world. Having also owned a couple of Ferrari Modena's, I must admit, Porsche isn't the only thrill car for rich showoffs and sports car buffs.

Later, when Porsche went public, having to satisfy shareholders demand for ever more profit, this greed helped produce the models 924, 928 and finally the Boxter, certainly no true Porsches when compared to a Carrera or a Turbo.

The difference in handling in precarious situations between a Porsche and a Ferrari was quite unnerving. When the Porsche started to break out you simply had to accelerate to bring in the back, typical for a rear engine car. The mid engine Ferrari, on the other hand, could only be corrected when it started to spin threatening to hit the oncoming traffic, by braking hard and letting ABS, anti lock brakes, more or less keep it in a somewhat straight line. However in the Swiss mountains, after a heavy winter that caused many potholes, the Ferrari would jump like a wild stallion and you had to control it well not to land in a ravine. In contrast, the Porsche took potholes in its stride.

Meeting the son of Ferdinand Porsche was one of the highpoints of my career and convinced me that hands-on management is the secret of success. It explains how Porsche became a world leader in automotive engineering.

If you apply the experiences with the German automotive industry to Detroit it is easy to understand why General Motors and Chrysler needed government bailouts. The greed of labor unions and top management's failures to curtail this unsupportable folly was mainly responsible. Perhaps Ford, still benefiting from the early family type management culture, knowing what happens on the factory floor, saved it from needing bailout funds.

In this context it is hard to understand why unions collect member fees primarily to support one political party rather than financing expert trade schools and taking a more balanced economic approach. No wonder, a once proud city, Detroit, is now mired in crime and widespread poverty. It probably could have become the automotive capital of the world if foreign car companies saw advantages in setting up operations there. Instead, they created jobs mainly in the South were union power is minimal.

Another example is Siemens, a once bureaucratic, client-needs ignoring, and state tolerated telephone monopoly, which started to face fierce private enterprise competition. It rapidly changed into a highly profitable, efficiently run corporation, spanning the world with its excellent products and services.

Working for all of these top financial institutions and the broad spectrum of companies from the major industrialized countries, I gained a deep insight into their diverse management philosophies and nationally shaped corporate cultures. Advising their leaders on matters of dealing with the press, presenting themselves on television, formulating speeches and consulting on mergers, acquisitions and takeovers, as well as organizing major receptions and press conferences, I was daily involved in dealing with the main target audiences, the public, the staff, governments and the journalistic community in the major countries.

At that time most journalists reported the news without letting their political beliefs dominate their style. Opinion was restricted to the editorial page, and columnists' contributions. There certainly has been a dramatic change with many journalists reporting the news… colored with their political slant today.

My company had grown in thirty years from a small three staff organization to a seventy member, medium sized company with offices in Frankfurt, Paris, and a holding in Geneva, with two subsidiary companies.

I sold a minority stake of my company to Burson-Marsteller, a subsidiary of Young and Rubicam, to gain more professional know how. As a result of this decision, I got to know and respect Harold Burson, one of the world's foremost authorities in public relations. He taught me crisis management and other decisive disciplines. His personal note, wishing me a happy eightieth birthday read: "Dear Eric. Happy Birthday! Please remember that 80 is the new 60. You're still a young man compared to me. With warm regards. Harold Burson". He was a sprightly ninety-two at the time of writing that message.

Having lived and worked thirty years in Germany, I decided it was time to retire and let younger people run the organization. The first step was planning to go public. It was a strenuous exercise dealing with lawyers, accountants and bankers, as well as making major presentations. We selected the Paris Bourse as the best place to list with Frankfurt being too expensive and Geneva too elitaire. The whole affair was extremely costly and diverted great resources from the entire staff. We started in early 2000 and the introduction of our shares was scheduled for October 8, 2001.

Shortly after the first day of trading the share price increased from around eight Euros to over twenty and on paper I was worth about twenty-two million Euros. The exuberance didn't last very long. Some of our large revenue clients were from Wall Street and with the September "9/11" 2001 U.S. national disaster; they suspended their contracts having to concentrate on U.S. priorities. I had to inform the shareholders of our drop in revenue and some of my best friends lost a great deal of money having bought our shares with confidence in our future. The share price dropped back to the issuing quote.

These adverse developments deeply affected my health and I suffered a severe nervous breakdown with devastating side effects. My time was up after our largest company in Frankfurt had to go into bankruptcy. I carefully planned my suicide, driving my Ferrari into the garage and closing the door; the exhaust gases were to finish the job. Fortunately, I seemed to hear a voice that reminded me that it was not my life and I had no right to end it. After this life changing drama, I slowly recovered and decided to return to my favorite country, America, were I was given the best chances of my career and enjoyed my most memorable days.

During that difficult period in my life I always carried a pocket sized Italian Bible with me which gave me great comfort. I also had to learn the hard way how you can indeed control your mind.

My wife, a God gifted artist all her adult life, was of great help getting me back on my feet. Luckily, she had decided years earlier to settle in St.Petersburg, Florida, a jewel of a most charming city with a climate that can only be described as ideal.

Without the daily challenges and stress of my own business, having only to take care of myself, I had to get adjusted to being retired. I could not see myself enjoying the beach, golf, or tennis; or watching television every day without some more definite commitment. After volunteering for some jobs, I finally decided to start a new career in the computer business of which I knew very little. Luckily, a certified Microsoft engineer agreed to help me get on my feet and I was able to start on a journey of new challenges, meeting hundreds of mostly kind people that needed help with their computers.

All of these meetings encouraged me to write another book, after the success of my first one about Germany which is still selling on Amazon for a decent, sometimes, very high price. I choose the title "My America, Wake-up! Be Proud," which reflects my personal sentiment about my adopted country.

Chapter 5

Banking and Beyond

As an advisor and consultant to large financial institutions, medium sized regional banks as well as private banks and mutual funds mainly in Germany, Switzerland, Lichtenstein, France, Luxembourg, and to a lesser extent in the UK and the US, I gained great insight into the banking business formulating introductions to their annual reports, writing speeches, organizing press conferences, assisting in publicity for mergers, acquisitions and public offerings as well as crisis management and organizing major receptions.

As in any other business there are conservative and honest leaders in banking, but some executives and traders in big and small banks are misusing their power, giving tainted advice to investors to get rid of risky shares and paper they do not want to hold themselves.

A typical example is what the financial community, their analysts and traders did with Lucent shares after they became a much liked stock by the pros, increasing from around nine dollars to over eighty dollars in the late 1990s. When analysts of one of the biggest mutual funds became aware that the stock was highly overpriced, they dumped hundreds of million of dollars worth of shares. The bankers and traders had to buy! After all, the fund was one of their biggest clients. It was absolutely clear to these buyers that the share price was going to nose dive and they had to get rid of their holdings as fast as possible.

They revved up their publicity, touting this stock as a promising investment to their private clients and less informed foreign bankers. One of my acquaintances in a remote village in Switzerland received a call from his local banker advising him to buy Lucent stock. He lost around eighty percent on this investment. This was a prime case of "insider trading." However, the regulatory authorities tacitly overlooked this typical insider trading activity, going after the book manipulating executives of Lucent instead.

Having made speeches on the elasticity of the insider trading regulations, I have always been amazed how regulators usually select and convict high profile individuals such as Martha Stewart or Christian Nordgren, leaving the big and powerful insiders in peace. Christian Nordgren was the chief executive of the exclusive Bank in Lichtenstein and at the same time he was on the board of a large Swedish company that was planning a take over of an American company. I am confident that he did not think of insider trading when he bought shares of this company having assumed that the takeover was already known. I knew him well for his bank was one of our big clients. The Bank secrecy of Lichtenstein did not protect him. The Americans forced the bank to disclose the name. Bernard Madoff was also singled out and convicted while the big schemers were not persecuted. "He who wields the power calls the shots."

In this context it is worth mentioning that the Swiss caved in after the American authorities demanded they should drop their claim to secrecy as far as American citizens are concerned. The authorities had a lethal weapon, the threat to close their subsidiaries in the U.S. if they didn't give in. The U.S. is the only nation that succeeded in breaking the Swiss banks' secrecy law, dating back to 1934.

In the interim, the Swiss secrecy law has been watered down providing information in criminal cases. Of course, American authorities consider tax evasion a crime. If this principle were harshly applied in some other countries a large number of their citizens would land in jail.

Banks claim they have an iron curtain between their analyst, merger and acquisition departments and their traders. This is nothing more than a convenient smokescreen covering up front-running and other illegal practices. Front-running, which is widely practiced, is trading equity on information from the analyst department before clients have the same information.

A front page story in *The Wall Street Journal* singled out another bank scheme: selling highly speculative shares in an initial public offering, IPO, without advising investors of the inherent risks. The banks make their profit on fees and front-running before a public offering. A top IPO manager got accused, but a hung jury set him free.

This double standard became even more apparent to me when the German authorities were investigating me about insider trading. My case was simple and straight forward. I advised the chief executive of a mostly family owned, medium sized company how to deal with the press after the share price dropped dramatically as a result of much lower priced imports. Meanwhile, one of my managers gained information about an impending acquisition, after the accompanying bank asked for public relations support. Watching the share price of all my clients every day, I suddenly noticed that the price of my client's shares rose steadily with a higher than usual volume.

I remembered the book of a Barron's editor entitled: "Buy Low, Sell High." He explained that if a stock starts to rise with a higher than usual volume, someone knows something that is not widely known. He advised to watch the stock a couple of days, then buy and sell after a gain of about twenty percent. I applied this rule and bought the stock of my client on the assumptions that some people knew something I wasn't aware off. I explained my actions to the regulators and implied they should investigate bank trading before the news broke instead. They dropped my case and bank insiders were never questioned. The top executive of my client was conveniently, accidentally, shot on a hunting expedition, obviously by some furious friends who lost a great deal of money.

Bank failures, and there are many world-wide, is another subject worth looking into. If every banker was forced to read the independent and excellent research readily available from the Bank of International Settlements, headquartered in Basel Switzerland, some failures could possibly be avoided. They make it clear that risky speculation with low margins is a major factor as well as insecure mortgage lending. Another cause for failure is manipulating the books. With bank clients asking for higher returns and shareholders demanding better profits, this greed inevitably leads some bankers into riskier investments. However, the basic rule applies: "the higher the return the bigger the risk."

The Bank of International Settlements, BIS for short, was founded in 1930. It is owned by the central bankers of the world. The bank advises and gives counsel to these owners. It has no private clients and isn't beholden to any one Central Bank or the Federal Reserve. It gives input on regulations, liquidity; inter-bank activities and other important subjects. It encourages reserve transparency and shares information on asset inflation bubbles among its many activities.

Speculation and manipulation is wide spread. I had my own experience with one of my company's clients The Herstatt Bank, headquartered in Cologne, Germany. The bank maintained a small branch network in the rich industrial Ruhr area. Its cofounder and personal liable partner Iwan D. Herstatt was a highly respected private banker, a towering personality. The bank flourished until he became senile and the younger generation took over. I made a lunch appointment with the new chief executive to secure our small business of public relations and advertising. My guest informed me that he was going to cancel our contract since he was closing his branch network and thus had no more need for public relations, or advertising.

He explained that his traders under the guidance of Danny Dattel made more profit in a couple of months than all of his branches in one year. Since he was my client, I couldn't call him a fool, if he had confidence in this casino like trading in derivatives.   Warren Buffet, the sage of Omaha, comes to mind with his comment: "Derivatives are financial weapons of mass destruction."

That bank went bankrupt shortly after we published their last annual report and Iwan Herstatt died soon thereafter a broken man having been accused of fraud and manipulation of the books. This bank failure made world headlines since many major foreign banks incurred heavy losses, and this adverse trading situation is still referred to as "The Herstatt Risk."

Another example is the demise of one of the oldest private banks in the UK, Baring Brothers whose owners became victims of a gun slinging young bluffer, who started as a bank clerk and rose to the stature of a gigantic hoaxer speculating billions in derivative trading. Fortunately he landed in jail, but the bank failed.

That a leading Swiss Bank gets fined a couple of billion dollars for manipulating the inter bank rate, LIBOR, reflects the dubious characters of some of these greedy bankers. The usually active investigating journalists are pretty subdued in these cases; after all, banks are a big advertising clientele of their employers. The losers are the shareholders and the bank's clients. The perpetrators of these frauds go free or are retired with a golden parachute.

The Swiss finally took action and introduced legislation to let shareholders vote on separation payments and bonuses. This assures that executives no longer have the sole power to give themselves financial benefits without shareholders approval.

Another typical case of this power seeking, corrupt corporate culture was Merrill Lynch, at one time a substantial client of my company. I started out as a public relations advisor believing in their integrity and investment banking acumen. Their slogan "The Thundering Herd" seemed appropriate. Later, after getting to know more about their sales tactics, their commission structure and disdain for some clients, it seemed to me that the thundering herd wasn't aware of the abyss they were to stampede into. Their settlement with Orange County, California, of around four hundred million dollars, after being accused of selling risky investments without warning this big client, revealed their dubious attitude towards their small clients as well.

As the acclaimed leader in the market for CDO's, collateralized debt obligations, popularly referred to as mortgage backed securities, Merrill Lynch took full advantage of its large network with underwriting and sales power to place these overrated securities. The crash of the property market, however, broke the bull's back and laid bare their culture demonstrating little interest in the well being of their clients. The power to milk cash cows bred corruption and sped up the collapse of this once highly regarded investment house. The losers were their clients and shareholders while the top brass collected huge bonuses. A law here in the U.S. similar to the one in Switzerland makes great sense to avoid this misuse of corporate funds.

Another immense speculative force is the stock market. It can be a safe place to accumulate profits with cautious and researched trading, selling, by taking profits on a regular basis rather than letting euphoric greed control investment policies. The much admired mutual fund pioneer, Sir John Mark Templeton made some sophisticated comments about the market: "avoiding the herd" was one of his principles. He warned early about the asset bubble of the property markets. His much quoted opinion about the stock market: "Bull markets are born on pessimism, grow on skepticism, mature on optimism and die on euphoria," is well worth remembering when evaluating overall market trends.

The Great Depression of 1929 was a tragic lesson about what runaway euphoria will lead to. It was an immense collapse ruining the lives of millions of Americans. Stock prices tumbled when the masses tried to sell and no one was buying. The dream to become rich quickly forced many into bankruptcy. The run on banks to withdraw their cash holdings forced many banks to close. New Government regulations were put in place to avoid a similar disaster, but the advance of computerized trading on margin wasn't taken into account. It now is possible to trade huge volumes in seconds thus threatening an orderly market.

The crash of 1987 when record margin calls overwhelmed the system with the Standard and Poor, The S&P 500 index dropped a whooping twenty percent. Trading was temporarily halted while Alan Greespan, the Federal Reserve Chairman, provided almost unlimited liquidity to the banks that were financing the traders. This allowed traders to take up their normal activities of market making. Millions of investors lost fortunes punished by not following the rule to take profits on a regular basis in a bull market rather than hoping for ever larger gains. The greater the paper gains the higher the risk. It is hard to understand how smart investors rely on paper gains in the market to increase margin buying, or taking out another mortgage on the basis of the increase in value of their property. Shares, properties or any other assets return their true value only when being sold.

Speculation parallels are amazing and document the cause of failure. Take the example of mortgage backed securities. The rating agencies in cahoots with their owners gave these risky papers an AAA rating and many buyers believed this overt bank fraud.

Swiss and German bankers compared these securities to their own papers, Hypotheken in Switzerland and Pfandbriefe in Germany, which had overall a pretty good safety record.
They lost billions as did many major banks all over the world.

Again, the journalist only briefly mentioned this major fraud and the authorities let small banks fail, but bailed out the big perpetrators of this scheme. Thomas Jefferson, who wrote the Declaration of Independence at the age of thirty three, commented: "I believe banking institutions are more dangerous to our liberties than standing armies."

After all, banks rank among the biggest contributors to politicians. Sandy Weil, the former Chairman of City Corp. made the point that big banks should be split up to avoid big failures in the future. He should know!

The study of bank failures always confirms the same pattern: the real estate boom in Switzerland during the 1980s was followed by a sharp drop: the banks incurred losses of around forty-two billion Swiss Francs, approx eight and a half percent of their entire loan portfolio How these same banks could fall for the fraudulent market of mortgage backed securities is hard to understand. Little or no market discipline, driven by greed, caused many bank failures in most European countries especially Spain, Sweden, Norway and Italy.

Canadian banks, on the other hand, being restricted in speculation, were not affected by the banking crisis of 2011. Where were the US regulators? Charles Christopher Cox, Chairman of the Securities and Exchange Commission during the Bush Administration warned Congress in a letter that investment banks with their holding companies in the Cayman Islands were totally unregulated and were able to hide some of their manipulations and speculations. Was the Federal Reserve Chairman, Alan Greenspan, unaware of the looming crisis? After all, his easy money policies were a leading cause of risky sub prime mortgage lending. Aesop, the Greek mystical writer of fables and philosopher wrote many years ago: "We hang the petty thieves and appoint the great ones to public office."

In that context the father of President John F. Kennedy comes to mind. "Joe" Kennedy, owned the largest office building in the country, Chicago's Merchandise Mart. Everything was and still is possible in this fair city and in the State of Illinois. It's widely believed he bought the necessary votes for his son to defeat Nixon with the help of the powerful political machine.

Currency speculation enabled George Soros to make his millions betting against the British Pound and other currencies. He is now able to support ultra progressive liberal causes as a so-called philanthropist. There are competent voices that recommend that Central Bankers should not only regulate interest rates and adequate liquidity, but they should also adjust currency parities. This would make the devastating speculation in currency futures impossible. However, Central Bankers can also make dramatic mistakes; Greenspan comes to mind and the head of the Bank of France who tried to back "Franc Fort" which turned out to be totally futile.

It is most unfortunate that Central Bankers always let the small banks fail while supporting the big and powerful ones. This was made clear to me, when my company organized a major reception in Frankfurt with a high profile speaker. As the owner of the company, I was sitting between the Central Banker from Switzerland and the German Central Banker whose son was working as a volunteer during summer vacation at my company. They made it quite clear to me that it was too dangerous to let a market leader fail since it would cause undue turbulence in world markets.

I doubt that this is a truly credible argument. Perhaps failure is not the answer, but breaking up the monolithic giants may be a better course of action. Bank of America is a typical example. It has already been bailed out twice, but their top executives haven't learned much from their past mistakes. The corporate culture has remained the same. The mess they made out of foreclosures is a tragedy for millions of homeowners which prudent lending could have avoided, but commission gains were too tempting and many clients were seduced to take on too much debt to finance their dream property.

Accumulating wealth has a lot to do with patience. My first Porsche, a 356, cost me DM ten thousand seven hundred Deutsche Marks. It would now fetch over two hundred thousand U.S. dollars. I bought my first cottage in the picturesque suburb of London, Richmond, a stone's throw away from the sprawling Richmond Park, for Pound Sterling 19,000; it was last sold for over a quarter million.

The same of course holds true for antiques, precious metals and even blue chips.

Chapter 6

The Environment and Beyond

As a boy I was swimming regularly in the beautiful Lake of Lucerne, Switzerland, which in summer reached temperatures ranging from sixteen degrees Celsius to a maximum of twenty-three, around sixty-one Fahrenheit to seventy-four. Then one year all beach access was closed to the public, the lake was dying, no more fishing or bathing. It turned out that all the major lakes in and around Switzerland were completely polluted since the surrounding cities had no sewage disposal plants and their refuse drained into the lakes. Once the federal government stepped in, after numerous cases of Typhoid fever were also reported, sewage plants were installed everywhere and the lakes became again the clean, blue shining waters, full of healthy fish.

When I settled in London, in the late fifties, the Thames River was a filthy, brown, stinking water way and rats found their way into the kitchen of the noble Savoy Hotel, as was reported to me by my neighbor who happened to work in this kitchen. At the same time, around October and November it was not advisable to travel by car to a nearby restaurant for dinner. Dense smog made it impossible to find your way back, unless you followed a bus to the depot and then went home on foot. Finally, the government took action. The Thames was totally freed of pollution from upstream and once again became a healthy river. At the same time households and businesses were forced to use smokeless fuel only and the smog disappeared, turning into normal fog.

My experience in Germany in the late fifties was much the same. When I visited the highly industrialized Ruhr area, my white Porsche turned slightly red from the dust of copper mills after only a couple of hours parking. The Ruhr River was a filthy, smelly stream. The government finally introduced strict environmental protection regulations which were enforced with German efficiency, and the results were astounding.

Talking about German efficiency, I well remember when I had to go for governmental inspection with my new Porsche. The mechanic checked everything, but even though it was a completely new car it didn't pass, because one screw on the license plate was black instead of white. I had to go to a nearby garage to have it painted white and undergo another inspection. The police also regularly check the noise of motorbikes in relation to the legally established decibel level.

Magnificent Venice, Italy, was also mired in filth. The sea was disgustingly dirty in and around the city and the smell was foul. The authorities introduced much needed measures to contain pollution and the bad odor as well as the many rats disappeared, and the city became again a well worth tourist attraction.

Of course, the same was true in America where the Environmental Protection Agency has and still is doing a much needed job to contain pollution and secure the natural beauty of the country. Environmental consciousness, not taking nature for granted, using available resources with care, yes! However, creating guilt is the beginning of dictatorship!

All this progress was achieved without fear mongering by the press, and without dire predictions by scientists who were vying for government research funds. A typical example was the highly exaggerated scare of the dying forests as a result of acid rain. *Life Magazine* ran a color spread of the barren larch trees surrounding the world renowned resort of St. Moritz in Switzerland as a typical example of the horrid impact of acid rain. I was staying at the luxurious Palace Hotel at the time and checked with the concierge about this natural disaster. He smiled and lectured me that this had nothing to do with acid rain, but was a natural occurrence every seven years when a moth called Zeiraphera griseana devours all greenery on the larch trees.

Media frenzy was supposedly caused by the disappearance of the ozone layer protecting the earth from deadly sun rays. Today, there is no more news about that. At the time the use of hairsprays was banned ignoring the fact that natural underwater volcanic eruptions and cows produce a much higher volume of the same dangerous gases.

Finally, now we are bombarded with the news about the inherent dangers of global warming. The intellectual pygmy, Al Gore, is in the forefront of this money making scam. All these experts have to do is study the climatic history of the earth over the last few thousand years to know this is irrelevant. There were always enormous volcanic eruptions with scorching heat creating mountains, lakes and islands, and moving entire continents. There was a recorded ice age and scientific research, drilling in the Artic ice, revealed great temperature changes over thousand of years.

Obviously, the world gets warmer around major population centers, but global warming is a speculative myth. In fact, the highest recorded temperature at LAX Airport was 110 degrees F in 1963. Humans know little about the sun's eruptions and their consequences and nature's supreme powers. A visit to Yellowstone Park can teach a great deal about the volcanic interior of the earth. The earth crust there is wafer thin and hot geysers and boiling ponds document the immense heat. Earthquakes, hurricanes, tsunamis or other natural disasters should teach humans to be more humble when trying to predict accurately global climatic trends.

Chapter 7

Religion and Beyond

My mother was a Protestant and my father a non practicing Catholic, being a successful politician and leading publisher, he took issue with the politics of the Vatican. I was baptized a Protestant in a predominantly Catholic community and soon realized that I was an outsider. Hence, I decided to attend Catholic Catechism classes and greatly enjoyed the outstanding wisdom of these teachings.

Later in life, after studying the history of the Catholic Church, the persecutions of the non-believers, the intrigues, the politics and yes, the crimes, I became a know-it-all atheist. After all, I was an arrogant student and usually first or second in my favorite disciplines. However, it only took a few years more and I turned into a convinced agnostic.

Eventually my religious belief took a dramatic turn when I had numerous occasions to experience the presence of a Supreme Being which most people call God. However, when I saw the widespread

76

misuse of the word "God" by sect leaders, corrupt television preachers and religious scam artists, I called myself a deist, a strong believer in a Supreme Being, but not accepting, nor denying the Trinity. The word deist derives from the Latin "deus," the literal translation meaning God. Deism is defined as the belief that using normal reasoning… marveling at nature, its human and animal life, one must come to the conclusion that there is a Supreme Being.

Most major religions have been established, are administered and are still dominated by males. The Bible's subtle suggestion of male supremacy has helped to deny women's access to the hierarchies of most religions and some even suppress and deny them basic human rights. I believe there is also another reason. Women mostly shun philosophy because it concentrates on argumentative logic with men dominating this field, while women use logic but also emotion and empathy guided reasoning. In fact, most men in power are afraid of women because they do not accept a lemming like following, but are willing to question the alpha male's dictates.

The arrogance of men to largely ignore women philosophers such as Aristoclea, 6th century BC, Anne Louise de Stael, Simone Weil to name a few, or Simone de Beauvoir, life companion of the French existentialist philosopher, Jean-Paul Sartre speaks volumes of men's clan like behavior. Sartre was awarded the 1964 Nobel Prize in Literature, but he refused it, commenting: "A writer should not allow himself to be turned into an institution."

On the humanitarian side of religion, women have indeed accomplished a great deal. Mother Theresa is preeminent, with her comment: "By faith, I am a Catholic nun." This statement gives credit to the thousands of nuns that perform selfless tasks every single day, helping the poor and the suffering, while the Vatican engages in power struggles and intrigues.

One such example, of many, is the reign of the wealth manager on behalf of the Vatican, Cardinal Paul Marcinkus from Chicago, (where else), who in 1982 was implicated in financial scandals, especially the collapse of the Banco Ambrosiano whose chairman was Roberto Calvi. Journalists, such as David Yallop for his book "In God's Name" and Mino Pecorelli were also investigating the involvement of Marcinkus and Calvi with organized crime. Conveniently, Calvi was found hanging on Blackfriars Bridge in London with the authorities suggesting it was suicide, while the Journalist Pecorelli was also found shot dead. Indeed, the dark forces did a fine job.

The sex scandals and their cover up tainted the prestige of the Catholic Church even more and many Catholics look askance at these developments calling themselves non-practicing Catholics as a result of the Vatican's moral decline.

All these negative aspects of the male hierarchy in the Catholic Church should not overshadow the good deeds and daily sacrifice performed by the many dedicated nuns and ordained priests. John XXIII, the much loved Pope, preached tolerance and understanding for your fellowmen, while the Saint Padre Pio helped hundreds with his healing powers and wise preaching.

Padre Pio's spiritual guidance included the following brilliant observation. Someone complained to Padre Pio of being distressed by sins he had committed. Padre Pio replied: "That which you feel is pride; it is the demon which inspires you with this sentiment, it is not true sorrow." The penitent replied: "Father, how can you then distinguish what comes from the heart and is inspired by Our Lord, and that which instead is inspired by the devil?" "You will distinguish it," replied Padre Pio, "always by this: The spirit of God is a spirit of peace, and also in the case of grave sin, it makes us feel tranquil sorrow, humble, confident, and this is due precisely to His mercy. The spirit of the demon, on the contrary, excites, exasperates, and makes us in our sorrow feel something like anger against ourselves, whereas our first charity must be to ourselves, and so if certain thoughts agitate you, this agitation never comes from God, who gives tranquility, being the Spirit of Peace. Agitation comes from the devil."

The mystic of the Catholic Churches, their artistic frescos, their huge stained glass windows that beam the sun's rays in magnificent splendor into the saintly ornate interior, the towering organs that thrill with soothing music, the raised pulpits, wherefrom the priests talk down to the believers, reflect the intricate, heart warming manipulation of the masses.

If only the hierarchy of the Church would be more humble, less doctrinaire, allowing women to help guide their future, with priests and nuns enjoying marriage, the Catholic religion could march on into a brighter future.

Some religions subjugate women in the name of God and practice outrageous atrocities against mankind, substantiating the French philosophers' Blaise Pascal's comment. The religious wars bear ample testimony to these corrupt, power hungry, fake prophets.

In every speech Adolf Hitler shouted: "God stands behind us," while his henchmen persecuted Jews, the Romani People, often referred to as Gypsies, deserters and the mentally ill. Could it be that his dark forces were afraid of the often superior intelligence of the Jews, documented throughout history, debunking Hitler's dream to create a Nordic Aryan master race? The vast Jewish influence in Wall Street, in Hollywood, in science and commerce, documents their advanced intelligence.

Mayer Amschel Rothschild of German Ashkenazi Jewish origin, born, 1744, in the Ghetto of

Frankfurt, referred to as the "Judengasse," is a typical example of this Jewish acumen. He rose from a modest beginning as a money changer to the foremost banker in Europe spreading his empire with his five sons running the family banks in the European financial centers. At the beginning he entered the City of Frankfurt from the Ghetto each morning, trading and selling on a stool in a big park, called today the Rothschild Park. The Rothschild bankers became the most successful business family in history accumulating the largest fortune in the modern world. Historians, however, mostly ignore the important role of the Rothschild family in the nineteenth century.

The Jewish faith is based on the Hebrew Torah and Tanakh as a deist, monotheistic, religion. It claims a special relationship God established with the children of Israel. Judaism has flourished for more than three thousand years and it has greatly influenced Western ethics as well as civil law. It has no supreme leader like the Pope, but authority is vested in the holy texts that are interpreted by rabbis and scholars. It is a fine religion honoring human dignity, strong family ties and deep traditions strengthened during centuries of enduring hatred and persecution.

An acquaintance of mine, a 92 year old distinguished Jew, asked me why I thought Jews had been persecuted throughout centuries. I answered with the following story: as a boy my family lived on a street were there was a big, beautiful house with a large white fence occupied by a wealthy Jewish family. Every working day, two Jewish boys came to our school, differently dressed with their little caps. They were much smarter than we were and never played with us. We didn't hate them, but we didn't particularly like them. To us they were strangers. My acquaintance smiled humouredly and commented: "You are very close, we are indeed strangers, in fact, we are aliens, you must have heard about the Hebrew tribe in Africa and nobody knows how they got there." Quite a thought! The fact is that many Jews have a greater identification with the Universe, rather than only with the Earth, and they can more readily receive and absorb knowledge that is all embracing in the Universe.

But there are not only Jewish men that document these formidable abilities. Hedwig Maria Kiesler, the only child of Jewish parents, made the first, sexually explicit film, "Exstasy," which brought her immense fame, but also severe criticism. With her husband, who had close ties with the Nazi regime, she attended scientific discussions about weapons guiding systems pretending to be a stupid actress. In fact, she was a brilliant mathematician and inventor, with unrivalled mental agility and capacity. When the Nazis started to persecute Jews, she immigrated to the U.S. and became known as Hedy Lamarr. She invented the wireless guiding system which was patented and used by the U.S. Navy years after in 1942.

There is a small minority of atheists that claim to know that there is no God. I consider them dangerous, because they try to force a majority of decent, upright believers to stop praising God in public, in schools, and in government bodies as well as during the Holy Season. They undermine the moral fabric of society and try to replace it with empty, self -centered phrases. Many are active as journalists and pundits in influential media outlets as well as in the cultural center, Hollywood, which is becoming more and more a godless, sexist, violent Gomorrah. On the other hand, I respect atheists that believe there is no God for they are mostly tolerant and refrain from imposing their belief on others.

The much admired Albert Einstein commenting on his religious conviction said: "I believe in Spinoza's God who reveals himself in the orderly harmony of what exists, not in a God who concerns himself with the fates and actions of human beings." Baruch Spinoza was a Jewish-Dutch philosopher in the sixteenth century, a great rationalist whose books were banned by the Catholic Church. Einstein went on to comment: "I do not believe in a personal God. If anything is in me which could be called religious then it is the unbounded admiration for the structure of the world so far as science can reveal it."

As long as the majority of Americans believe in God, America, the beautiful, will remain a strong and morally leading nation, a shining star for the entire world.

Chapter 8

Health, Addictions and Beyond

As a young boy, every year the school dentists checked our teeth and most pupils could have them fixed by the same dentist. However, since my father's income exceeded the set limit, I had to go to a private dentist. The selected expert filled my whole mouth with Amalgam and seventy years later my teeth are still in good condition. I tried to have them cleaned in Germany about fifty years later, but the dentist refused claiming the Amalgam had to be removed first. The cost would have been around DM twenty-five thousand. Using a Waterflosser and an electric toothbrush daily, I hope to enjoy healthy teeth for another few years without any visits to the dentist. Of course, the Amalgam scare was an excellent money maker for all the dentists.

Our family doctor was a tough, old lady, who drove an open convertible, even in late fall, while she was already well over eighty years old. She knew our family's history, insisted on a healthy diet, prescribed teas and herbs; and pills only in an absolute emergency. Our daily food consisted

86

mainly of vegetables coming directly from the government ordered maintenance of a small plot of land, and fruit came from trees in the neighborhood. There were little or no imports due to the war, hardly any sugar, coffee, rice or other exotic items. Healthy nutrition was the cardinal rule, and you only visited the doctor when you were seriously ill. Otherwise my mother gave us some herbs, berries or made some tea to cure our ills. She got the necessary advice from a priest she visited regularly up in the mountains.

Comparing the countries I have lived in for many years, I believe Americans swallow more pills than any other nationality. They even feed young kids with pills to calm them down or to correct Attention Deficit Hyperactivity Disorder. Well, I always suffered from ADHD when an attractive female was nearby. Most of these pills that interfere with the brain's normal functions, such as anti depressants have many as yet unknown side effects, and it is hard to understand why parents aren't more careful with these drugs. The Pharmaceutical Industry is not allowed to advertise prescription drugs in Switzerland as well as in some other European countries and the constant barrage of these messages is happily absent. Listening to the possible side effects, I will never understand how so many people swallow all these drugs, unless, of course, it is an absolute necessity. The advertising refrain: "Ask you doctor," sounds professional, but is misleading, since most doctors have little or no time and every visit costs money.

A typical example is the intake of sleeping pills. All of these pills interfere with the normal functioning of the brain, putting it more or less to rest. Eventually, the brain
begins to sleeps during waking hours as well and the most common side effect for the elderly is loss of memory. Why not drink a relaxing herbal tea or enjoy a couple of glasses of red wine instead?

I have some acquaintances who take upwards of ten drugs a day and rather than feeling better, they are getting worse, while the cost to the State is in no relationship to the so called benefits.

In summary, I would like to observe, that most Americans go to the doctor to find out that they are sick, while a typical Swiss goes to the doctor when he feels sick. The adverse effect of this habit is amplified by the comment of a professor of medicine, who stated: "The most common cause of illnesses is over diagnostics in the pursuit of health." Many of the recommended tests and shots are anything but fully accurate, or effective, and it is up to the doctor to interpret the results. If he has the patient's interest in mind, all is well; if however, the objective is to make money, the patient will suffer.

While living in Germany for thirty years, I decided to go for a yearly check up after fifty-five. The clinic I selected was highly recommended and the top surgeon became almost a personal friend. I passed all the tests with flying colors, except he diagnosed that my heart was a little on the weak side. A few years later, the clinic installed new, computerized test equipment, where the expert could follow the entire flow of the patient's blood. My tester spent a considerable length of time and finally announced: "I have some bad news, you need a heart bypass." I countered: "I feel great and nobody is going to operate and weaken me." He was rather upset and silently put my file in my folder.

The top surgeon checked my file, as always, and asked: "Anything in your family about hearts?" I pointed out, not that I knew of, but I called my brother. He informed me that he had a valve that didn't shut completely, but that this wasn't a major problem, unless he needed a complete blood transfusion, at which time absolutely clean blood was a necessity. My good acquaintance smiled and commented: "No operation is necessary, but it confirms my earlier diagnosis when I heard a slight murmur." After a brief pause, he added humorously: "This new machine cost us close to a million, and it must be amortized."

Another experience I had in Germany revealed the weakness of a system when the experts are driven by greed. At a bar I visited regularly in Dusseldorf where access was limited and entry was only possible with a face check by the owner, I met a gynecologist who invited me to his home having planned a major party. I happen to sit between two gynecologists at his gathering while they were discussing how many active patients each one got by referral following the death of one of their colleagues. I inquired what they meant by active. They explained, after a few drinks, that those were patients who were told that they had a small, nonmalignant growth in their uterus which had to be observed within a six monthly interval. In fact, there was no growth, but the visits produced good, regular income. The worries of the patients were of no concern to these experts.

Most people don't trust car salesmen, politicians, bankers, or lawyers. Why they often trust doctors blindly, is difficult to understand. The cartel of the all powerful American Medical Association, the pharmaceutical industries and the FDA, The Federal Drug Administration in the U.S., is intimidating enough to put it mildly. Journalists generally shy away from stories about their abuse of power since their advertising clout and political impact is too encroaching. I know a woman that needs a daily dose of a drug that overcomes her deadly blood disorder. The drug costs eleven thousand dollars for a twenty-eight day supply. How this price can be justified is hard to comprehend.

Looking for a successful National Health System, some American politicians such as Paul Ryan turned to Switzerland to get some valuable input. The Swiss system demands universal coverage for all of its citizens. It is consumer driven and individuals have the choice between compulsory coverage at Sfr. four hundred and twenty per person per month, or private insurance at Sfr. seven hundred and sixty per months. The truly needy get local community help provided by the individual states, but not by the Federal Government. The means test is compulsory and helps greatly to avoid fraud. A ten percent personal contribution to all health services is required which also reduces unnecessary visits to the doctor and avoids often useless tests and shots.

Whereas the source of payments for health care, according to some available research, is over sixty percent from consumers in Switzerland in the U.S. it is only around twenty-three percent; the Government in Switzerland contributes no more than around twenty-five percent while in the U.S. it is close on forty-five percent. Employers in Switzerland contribute no more than around six percent, but in the U.S. it is over thirty percent.

There is also a strict regulatory framework stipulating the prices doctors may be paid for their services, and injury awards are firmly set by the government rather than clever lawyers. The choice of insurance companies is exceedingly broad for the size of the market, with some Swiss insurance companies operating world wide and Swiss Re being one of the foremost re-insurers in global markets.

These vast differences highlight two major factors; The Swiss, guided by the tradition of their founding fathers, abhor centralized government and no political party is dominant. The health system is a compromise between the centre left and centre right, not as wrongfully reported in the U.S., by the conservatives and the liberals. The Liberal Party in Switzerland of which my father was a driving force, is the largest political grouping and it represents the center right, with the word liberal deriving from the Latin word "liber", meaning free. How liberal ever came to denote the Democratic Party in the U.S., which is for more government control rather than less, is a mystery. I guess it is like the word communism, which is being misused by communist parties, when in fact they embrace dictatorship.

The evolvement of how the government should treat abortion is another interesting example of how National Health developed in Switzerland. A long,

long time ago men poured absinthe, a distilled, highly alcoholic beverage, into the pregnant woman that desired an abortion. Some died of alcoholic poisoning, and some had a successful abortion. The Government stepped in and prohibited the sale of absinth. The result was that illegal abortion butchers set up shop outside major cities and ruined many lives of healthy young women who wanted to terminate pregnancies. Finally, the Government decreed that any adult woman could get an abortion during early pregnancy, but only an accredited doctor could perform the operation. At his discretion, he could also intervene at a later stage if the patient's life was in danger. That solved a major problem.

A similar positive change was introduced with the control of prostitution. In some European countries it is now regulated with the women having to register, pay taxes and visit the doctor regularly. The crime ridden activity spreading disease was thus legalized and accepted as a necessary part of society, even though many moralists decried these solutions. The colorful red light district in Amsterdam and Hamburg are typical examples.

Today, with the introduction of the pill and much less inhibited sexual behavior, the moral standards are in a steady decline, and the mysticism of sex is being replaced by a public display of hedonism. Pop tarts are featured on the covers of magazines; and in extensive media coverage they are presented as idols to the young. According to my knowledge of the English language a "tart" is a whore. One does not have to be a prude to wish for a more refined public stance. Of course, with the masses gobbling up stories about crime and sex, and the intrusive paparazzi hounding down decent princesses bathing topless or exiting a car in a short skirt, this salacious news is getting world-wide coverage and readership. The disadvantages of a free, rather than a responsible, press become obvious.

Some of the major addictions such as alcohol, sex, gambling, and drugs have always played a decisive role in human behavior and destroyed many a successful career, or even entire societies.

My encounter with addiction gave me some insight into their inherent dangers. It started with gambling. At the age of eighteen, I got my first car, an Italian

Topolino, a lovely toy of a compact vehicle. I planned a visit to the beautiful South of France during my summer vacation. Near Monte Carlo, I was flagged down by a handsome, older gentleman. I stopped and inquired what he wanted. He asked me if I was looking for a reasonably priced room to stay. When I agreed, he got into my car and directed me to a grand villa close to the sea. He explained that he was a professional gambler and that he had run out of luck and needed to rent some of his rooms for income. The price was right, the company interesting, and the location superb.

He convinced me to join him in a visit to the impressive Casino in Monte Carlo the next day and asked me to put up a couple of hundred Francs for gambling. We had an impressive winning streak, following his rather complicated system. After we won thousands, we went for an exclusive dinner, and I already saw myself driving home in a luxury car. The following day, we divided up the winnings and he suggested we play two tables at the same time with me also applying his system. We lost everything, and I didn't even have enough money left to return home. We now both flagged down tourists and finally, a German couple on their honeymoon came to check out the rooms. They agreed to stay and the owner convinced the young husband to go gambling with him the next day, while I went swimming with his wife. I told her of my loss, and she lent me enough money to be able to drive back home the same day.

After that experience, whenever I visited a casino anywhere in the world, including tempting Las Vegas, I always took only a few dollars in my pockets and if I won, fine, and if I lost, I called it a day. I enjoyed many a memorable evening in magnificent places. At the casino in Evian, on the Lake of Geneva, one of my close acquaintances lost a lot of money. But as a highly respected citizen, the banks lent him more at usury rates until one day he committed suicide and a colorful, happy human being was destroyed by this all consuming addiction.

An uncontrollable sex drive can also be highly destructive. Many a respected businessman or politician risked his marriage, hurt his children and lost his job over a brief love affair. In some countries, like Italy and France, the public, in general, and many women are more tolerant of a man's infidelity, considering it more of a peccadillo rather than a major character flaw. In as much as there is little doubt that the sex drive of males also stimulates the power drive, it follows that successful men are more prone to be unfaithful, especially since some women prey on the rich and help matters along. Tiger Woods, Governor Schwarzenegger and General Patraeus, are some typical examples of those having succumbed to this addiction.

Kings had harems, some religions accept bigamy; and some tribal leaders proudly present their many wives, all of which bears ample testimony to the polygamous nature of many males. This hard to control drive becomes immensely dangerous when it hurts other human beings as is the case with rape, pedophilia and other sexual aberrations.

Alcohol is another addiction that can bring disaster to a human life, even killing another person in a drunken driving accident. I had my own personal experience as a young man when there was still little traffic in Switzerland. I regularly borrowed my father's company car without his knowledge and one evening, under the influence, I hit a lamppost with the lights going out on a large stretch along the Lake of Zurich. The car was a total write off. I didn't dare to go home; the newspapers reported the accident and my parents were afraid I was injured. My brother finally found me, and brought me home, and I remembered for the rest of my life the inherent danger in drinking and driving. For many, the first mistake can be the last one. I was just lucky.

My only experience with drugs happened in Hong Kong. I was having dinner with a lively stewardess who put some drug into my drink while I went to the restroom. I was high for a good twenty-four hours. It felt exhilarating and I believed I could accomplish anything. When I sobered up, I became fully aware of the dangers of drugs and I never wanted to go on such a trip again. The temptation to use drugs is powerful and it is no surprise that so many, including athletes, are becoming addicted. If only they realized the ultimate price they will have to pay for their weakness.

Society should differentiate between criminal and self inflicting addiction. The latter should be treated with understanding, providing help, while the former should be punished harshly.

It is sad to notice, how few doctors put their emphasis on the vital importance of nutrition to the human body when advising their patients. Many Americans wolf down fast food coming out of the microwave, having been bought frozen. There is convincing evidence that the microwave destroys the nutritious value of food, documented in much credible scientific research. Luckily, some major food chains are starting to offer lower calorie and healthier food which is excellent news.

Chapter 9

My Beautiful America

Traveling to Italy as a boy with my father, I fell in love with that country. I liked the stupendous scenery, the Italians attitude toward life, their close family ties, their excellent food and their many historic cities with hundreds of monuments and awe inspiring cathedrals. Years later, after selling my company, I built two interconnecting luxury houses ten minutes from the Italian border, in the South of Switzerland, so I could enjoy dinner in the small Italian town of Tirano. Shopping in this picturesque city was a gourmet's delight. Delicate wines, juicy, marbleized beef, ripe cheese, goat and lamb, as well as a wide choice of antipasti made it a joy to prepare a fine meal.

Unfortunately, the Swiss Tax Authorities didn't accept my status as an American citizen, because I was a native born Swiss. They demanded high taxes on all the funds I brought into Switzerland, whereas as an American I wouldn't have had to pay any taxes. I decided to sell everything and leave for the

U.S.A. It was the right decision. America was always my first choice for business opportunities and my second choice for vacations.

Many Americans travel all over the world, visiting famous historical sites, enjoy culinary adventures and getting to know the touristy aspect of the nations they visit without having a chance to familiarize themselves with the country's everyday life. Unfortunately, equally, many do not fully appreciate the inherent beauty of America and the immense variety of historic sites and vacationing opportunities in their own country.

America has attracted immigrants from all over the world for centuries, who brought many of their native country's traditions, special cuisine, strong family ties as well as religious beliefs with them. This broad base of America's population laid the foundation of its grandiose diversity. The unfettered ability to earn and acquire wealth also made America the most generous nation in the world, and powerful and rich donors enabled America's unrivaled cultural development.

America can pride itself in having more high quality museums than any other nation. Many rank at the top, world wide. The J. Paul Getty Museum in Los Angeles or the Guggenheim Museum in New York are typical examples of cultural investments by the wealthy. The Metropolitan Museum of Art in New York, the Smithsonian Museum, as well as the United States Holocaust Museum in DC, or the Museum of Science and Industry in Chicago bear ample testimony of the willingness of local leaders to further the cultural base.

In addition, state, city governments as well as wealthy donors have made it possible for the country to become the home of many leading symphony orchestras. The New York Philharmonic, The Boston, Chicago, Cleveland, Philadelphia and Minnesota Symphony Orchestras are some shining examples of this world leadership.

When it comes to entertainment, Hollywood enriched the world already when I was a boy with memorable films for the family such as Bambi, Mickey Mouse and Popeye. Later classical adventure films such as Gone with the Wind or Casablanca enchanted the audience, followed by the unrivaled Western genre with films, radio and television. Today's productions mostly glorify violence and sex, but fortunately there are some producers that make terrific films such as The War Horse or Lincoln.

I enjoyed many beaches around the world ranging from the lively Italian Riviera, the worldly Cote d'Azur on the Mediterranean coastline, the charming Spanish Costa Brava, Acapulco in Mexico, the huge selection of fantastic beaches in Australia, or the swinging Copacabana beach in Brazil.

However, only America can offer a kaleidoscopic variety of beaches with intrinsically different natural surroundings and ethnic backgrounds. The wonderful beaches in Hawaii are totally different from the glamorous beach in Miami, the unspoiled Fort Desoto Beach with its own charm or the pristine Siesta Key Beach in Sarasota. The U.S. Virgin Island, referred to as the little Caribbean Paradise, with its friendly Afro-Caribbean population, can offer soft white sandy beaches to satisfy any taste contrasting beautifully with the deep blue sea.

Whatever your sport …ranging from hiking, surfing, fishing, hunting, swimming or simply admiring the beauty of nature and its diverse wildlife, America has a greater array of facilities with its many natural parks, dominating mountains, lakes, historic sites, monuments and entertaining amusement parks such as Disneyland and Universal Studios than any other country.

When it comes to sports America has equally much to offer with baseball, football, hockey, boxing and car racing to name some of the most popular ones.

I have visited dozens of national parks such as Bryce Canyon with its tall hoodoos, the Arches, the Red Rock wonderland, Monument Valley, Yellowstone and Yosemite Park. Yellowstone was so fascinating that I visited this mammoth park three times. I was impressed with its crystalline lakes, steaming geysers and impressive waterfalls. I watched the free roaming bison, the elks and some grey wolves. A close encounter with a grizzly heightened the adventure and black bears came within touching distance of the car.

The immense vastness of the park with its colorful flora and the many different birds, like hawks and eagles, are serene reminders of the inherent beauty of nature and the divine design of our earth and its myriad of creatures.

When I first arrived in the U.S., I visited a friend in Chapel Hill, North Carolina. The charm of this lovely city and the friendliness of its citizens gave me a memorable impression of southern hospitality and it doesn't surprise me that Chapel Hill ranks today in the top-ten best places to live in the nation.

After having built my own business, I could afford some luxurious trips and vacations in the States. A few days' stay at a top hotel such as The Pierre in New York, the iconic U.S. flagship of Taj Hotels, was an unforgettable high-life treat. Strolling down Fifth Avenue, visiting the large stores and smaller specialty shops on the side streets, was a shoppers dream. The huge selection of excellent restaurants always made a trip to New York a gourmet's delight. Broadway with its renowned theaters rounded up a full day of sightseeing with a great play or a musical.

A trip to Los Angeles was always filled with great entertainment, savoring succulent food, and sipping an Espresso at an elegant café on Rodeo Drive. It was a true pleasure for the palate as well as the eyes, watching mostly attractive people sashaying from shop to shop.

My visits to the West rekindled my memories of my youthful fantasy about the Wild West and its many illustrious as well as criminal characters. Cody in Wyoming put me back in history. It is a colorful western town with historic traditions. The magnificent Buffalo Bill Historical Center features colorful memorabilia of the West. Its displays of Indian culture pay homage to proud tribes, and pictures of western life enrich a grandiose tour of the West as it once was. Of course, one also has to visit Irma's Hotel, where one can admire the beautiful bar which was a gift from the Queen of England to Buffalo Bill, who gave it to his daughter, Irma. Many Cody citizens dress for tourists in Western Gear, proud of their heritage and America.

The City of Jackson in Wyoming is famous for its spectacular scenery, upscale shopping and culinary delights such as a dinner at the Snake River Grill.

107

An adventurous boat ride on the Snake River shows unspoiled scenery at its best and confirms why America is immense, majestic and exiting.

In proud Montana, I immensely enjoyed the visit to the beautifully rebuilt Virginia City, once the booming capital of Montana during the gold rush around a hundred-and-fifty years ago. After the city became a ghost town, it was rebuilt with affection and pride. It is now a major tourist attraction with Western type saloons, shops filled with authentic goods and old artifacts, and Boot Hill Cemetery with the original hanging place. The neighboring town of Nevada City features a priceless collection of electric organs and is also totally rejuvenated to its original state. In Butte, Montana, also rebuilt, they were mining gold and silver and one could stroll thru old Butte savoring the atmosphere of a true Western small town. In charming Bozeman a visit to the Computer Museum opens up one's eyes to the spectacular development in the field of computerization.

A sharp contrast was the visit to fascinating Salt Lake City, the world headquarters of the often persecuted Mormons. The historic Temple Square impressed with its immaculate maintenance and natural beauty. The tour of the majestic Tabernacle was a serene experience, allowing me to admire the towering, colorful organ and marvel at the superb acoustic. To watch the film of the history of the Mormons was a brilliant example of professional public relations. In all, a visit to Salt Lake City is more than well worth it with the surrounding areas offering excellent sports activities and grand parks.

Magnificent Monument Valley located on the Arizona-Utah state line is another trip bringing back Western memories. Its gigantic sandstone butts, reaching up to the sky made the awe inspiring backdrop for many Western films, especially movies by the famous director John Ford with his unforgettable film "Stagecoach" starring John Wayne.

The historic train ride from Durango to Silverton, Colorado, along a winding river, thru tunnels, over viaducts, and narrow ravines in an open carriage pulled by a beautifully kept steam locomotive is another first-class adventure. It is enriched by modern, comfortable amenities and true Western hospitality. The Grand Imperial Hotel in Silverton, dating back to 1882, is a jewel of heartwarming graciousness. Exquisite restaurants such as the Diamond Belle Saloon in true western style, make a trip to these two cities a wonderful experience.

My most memorable Western experience is a two weeks' stay, over three years at an immaculately kept private ranch outside the charming City of Dubois, Wyoming, where Walt Disney maintained his own small landing strip to enjoy relaxing days at his ranch.

The ranch I stayed at with two friends was expertly run by a couple in their eighties. They were supported by a Swedish cowboy and his charming wife and an excellent cook with several college degrees. Their corral was open during the night for the horses to roam freely on the open plane, coming back for feeding in the morning. Those semi-wild horses were ours to ride for a full day through woods, brooks, up and down hills and galloping over sprawling fields.

One of their neighbors, a ranch woman on her own, woke up one morning seeing a Grizzly in her living room. She locked herself in the bathroom with her cell phone and called for help. That story reminded us that we were out in the Wild West and that we had to avoid contact with animals and refrain from smoking in the open. To soothe our horse riding sores, the cowboy administered the healing cream used for their horses claiming it was the best treatment available for riders as well.

To revel in American history, the West is an ideal vacationing place reminding us of the heritage that laid the groundwork for today's modern country.

Now I live in Tampa Bay, Florida, a kaleidoscope of the Good Life in tandem with excellent business and work opportunities. My new home is Saint Petersburg featuring an upscale down town waterfront with attractive outdoor restaurants, grills and bars. Nearby are the white sands of St. Pete Beach, lively Treasure Island and more exclusive Pass-a-Grill. A short trip lets you enjoy artsy Gulfport with great outdoor restaurants or you can immerse yourself in Greek culture with the sponge divers in Tarpon Springs. The bustling City Tampa, ranked as one of the best outdoor cities, offers culinary delights, several large museums, the family entertainment Busch Gardens and the impressive

Lowry Zoo. Tampa Bay is also the home of top sports teams with the cities exuding the flair of affluence.

The Tampa Bay climate is ideal with mild winters and tropical summers, often with lower temperatures and humidity than some of the big cities up north. A local phenomenon is the migration of "Snowbirds." These are residents from up North including Canada that maintain a second home in Florida adding greatly to the cultural diversity of Tampa Bay.

As a retiree, I cannot imagine a more blissful life than enjoying the Good Life in Tampa Bay.

After having enjoyed my spoiled youth in picturesque Switzerland for twenty-two years, I worked hard and lived fully in swinging London for fourteen years traveling all over the world. I spent thirty years in efficient and prosperous Germany running my own company. These were highpoints of my career, but my fourteen years in America crowned my life with an unshakable hope in a bright future for this beautiful country.

Chapter 10

About Marriage

The union between men and women has been called marriage in most civilized countries, and this should not change. The word "marriage" is imbued with many positive attributes and it would be sad to misuse this word for other unions. A union between two men or two women is perfectly acceptable and they should have all the legal rights enjoyed by married couples. They should be authorized to adopt children for they make mostly excellent parents, and society should accept this development. During the history of humankind such unions have always flourished. I do believe, however, that it is wrong for some proponents to make a public spectacle of their union borrowing from the rites of marriage, which should be left to the union between a man and a woman. Tolerance is the key word in these matters.

Young couples should realize that marriage is not an ongoing honeymoon, but rather a continuous striving for harmony. It is impossible to change a person's basic character except through domination, which is always harmful to a happy relationship. Divorce is often a result of a lack of empathy, tolerance and understanding; as well as financial discipline. It must also be remembered that men's behavior while wooing a partner is often different then during marriage. If infatuation at the outset doesn't evolve into true love, there is little chance of a successful union.

It is difficult to understand, how some women seek out only handsome, successful men for marriage, forgetting that success is often achieved thru the power drive which is closely coupled to the sex drive, thus increasing the chances of infidelity. Wealth and power come often with a desire to manipulate others, and conquering women is part of this lifestyle. John Kennedy, Arnold Schwarzenegger and Tiger Woods are such typical examples, and it is surprising that their spouses were not prepared for these escapades.

Successful, aggressive males often select the most attractive females with sex appeal; Paul Getty, Donald Trump and Hugh Hefner are in this category.

Some societies see these matters differently, were marriage is arranged by the father who selects the groom, often ignoring the feelings of his daughter. Some religions even support polygamy and some peoples consider infidelity merely a minor faux pas.

For many stars in Hollywood marriage is a temporary union. They swap partners on a frequent basis. The popular press reports these affairs as something quite normal, and many young people are easily swayed to believe that this behavior is cool, when in fact it often destroys human dignity.

A happy union between two people demands sacrifice, suppressing egotistical behavior, empathy, and tolerance. All are decisive.

Chapter 11

Dark Forces

The Dark Forces have been active throughout history, fed mainly by corrupt power, corporate and political infighting, hatred, envy, jealousy and insanity. They are an integral part of the human race and cannot be banished by legislation.

Assassinations of emperors, kings, business rivals and political foes have been widespread, and often the true perpetrators cannot be caught because a front man has been used, tempted with money, only to be shot by an unknown professional. Some recent partially unsolved killings demonstrate how the Dark Forces operate in the background.

Two top leaders in Germany, the Chairman of the Deutsche Bank, Alfred Herrhausen, and Juergen Ponto head of the Dresdner Bank, were killed in the 1970s, and it was never clearly established who plotted these assassinations, but obviously there existed some powerful enemies of these two financial leaders.

It is also very unlikely that Oswald acted alone to plan and kill President John F. Kennedy. It appears more like a true organized crime job which always follows a similar pattern. The same style was employed in the murder of the fashion mogul, Gianni Versace, who planned going public with his company, but some Dark Forces that financed him weren't very happy. These types of crooks always find some front fool that gets convicted, as was the case with the murder of Martin Luther King, who certainly had many powerful enemies.

The Oil Cartel, "The Seven Ugly Sisters" that dominated the oil industry from 1940-1970s, were not very happy with the rising star, Enrico Mattei. The boss of The Italian Fuel Trust, dared to go it alone with deals in the Middle East. He died in a mysterious plane crash probably caused by a bomb planted on his plane by the Dark Forces.

Olof Palme, The Prime Minister of Sweden, was shot down in Stockholm in 1986. His murder remains unsolved, but rumors circulated that wealthy weapons dealers were unhappy over the competition by Sweden with its large arms sales.

Dow Jones also had a run in with the Dark Forces. The typesetters, hard working, upright union members were being replaced by computers. The Union insisted that they stay at their jobs. They were bored reading magazines and newspapers all day long without performing any productive work. Dow Jones took some drastic steps and moved the entire printing plant and administrative staff to a small town in New Jersey, where the company was welcomed with open arms. The Dark Forces took revenge and blew up trucks that delivered *The Wall Street Journal*. An editor wrote a story about the crime ridden unions and received life threats which forced him to relocate.

Mass murder has regularly been committed under the guise of religious freedom. To annex territory automatic weapons were used to eradicate Native Americans. Hitler's killing machine revealed the true horror of insane leadership in subjugating other nations, and killing people considered enemies of his Super Race.

The many hangings and killings of innocent blacks in the Southern U.S. is another example of this. The terror of the Ku Klux Klan, a white supremacist organization, reveals the depth of human intolerance and hatred.

It is easy to understand that some of these victims find it hard to forgive and forget. Still today, many blacks dislike whites and vice versa. Many Jews are not too fond of Germans, and with a little tolerance one can understand these lasting dislikes, hoping that time will heal these deep wounds. If you see mostly young blacks wearing their trousers far below their waistline exposing their underwear and butt, it probably signals their distain for the white majority with the expression "kiss my … ." In addition, they probably believe it is sexually cool. Certain clothing has often demonstrated power, hatred or opposition as with the Gestapo uniform, The Ku Klux Klan's robes, the Flower Children and many others.

The mysterious death of Edmond Safra, the higly successful Jewish banker, is another example of the omnipresence of Dark Forces. He died, along with his nurse, by suffocating in a fire lit on purpose by his bodyguard, who claimed that he was overwhelmed by two masked men and that he lit the fire to trigger the elaborate security system. Safra's

Trade Development Bank in Geneva was a client of one of my subsidiary companies. He was well liked and his bodyguard greatly appreciated his job. He sold another of his banks, Republic National Bank of New York, to American Express, and a nasty legal battle ensued between the two parties. There were many that profited from his death, and while his bodyguard was convicted, his story was simply ignored. It is more convenient for authorities to get a conviction than engage in a never-ending fishing expedition.

The sudden death of the journalist who investigated the connection between the top executive of the Vatican Bank, Banco Ambrosiano, Roberto Calvi, dubbed "God's Banker" and organized crime was never solved. The hanging of Calvi on a London Bridge was conveniently classified "a suicide."

Real or imagined injustices to men can trigger the most violent reactions. The recent story of the former L.A police officer is a case in point. He claimed he was wrongfully accused of irregularities. His hatred turned into uncontrollable fury. That turned into insanity, which launched his killing spree. Many of my black acquaintances sympathized with his hatred, but didn't condone his violent actions.

Another black acquaintance is a former St.Petersburg police officer. He explained to me his feelings when he and his black fellow officers were not allowed to patrol in white areas; only in black districts. They felt discriminated against. In the black communities they were mainly confronted with disdain, whereas in the white districts they could at least expect some respect. He resigned in disgust, but kept his cool and built another career helped by his strong faith in God. Fortunately, the St.Petersburg police lifted this ban which set a precedent for other police departments throughout the Nation to treat black officers the same as whites.

For governments to contain the Dark Forces is a Herculean task. These forces hide in the underground and always find access to weapons, bribing their way to achieve their aim. This must be remembered when talking about gun control. Criminals usually get what they need and in the process the honest citizens get shortchanged. Tighter controls as to who should qualify to get a weapon is a move in the right direction, but it will never stop a person from getting insane later in life or when pushed to the extreme by some real or imagined injustice to commit mass murder.

Probably the most heinous crime committed by the Dark Forces was the destruction of the Twin Towers, the symbol of U.S. power and the headquarters of many well known Wall Street firms. The Towers also were occupied by many successful Jewish financial leaders. Around four hundred Jews were killed in the attack. It is well possible that the Dark Forces had help on the ground by fanatics who hate America. After all, an earlier attempt was made to blow up the Towers by terrorists from within the U.S.

Evil is unfortunately an integral part of human nature. This was witnessed with crowds cheering when Christians were thrown to the lions. Similarly, spectators enjoy watching a vicious bullfight. Padre Pio's definition of evil gives some useful guidance how to deal with it. In its extremes, evil must be destroyed. Fortunately, the Good always seems to succeed in the end and I have never read about a violent criminal or a vicious dictator that died in peace.

Chapter 12

Politics and Beyond

I have always taken a keen interest in politics, probably because my father was a prominent politician, a leading force in the Liberal Party. Thus, I experienced early the advantages this brought for me personally. In school and later in life, I was always treated with more respect than many others, the police ignored some of my minor offenses, and teachers were more tolerant of my often stubborn behavior.

Switzerland has been blessed by a deep-rooted contempt for centralization which was nurtured all throughout its history. It started with the foundation of the country in 1291 by three Alpine states which swore The Oath of Confederation, a bond of brotherhood, to act jointly if their freedoms were threatened by outside aggressors. With four official languages and many different dialects; seven Chief Executives and a largely ceremonial President, elected for one year only; and twelve political parties, four of which are dominant; every political decision has to be a compromise. This assures that the Central Government cannot usurp too much power which often stymies a healthy economic and political development.

The European Union (EU), a closely knit economic and political union of twenty-seven member states, is the very antidote of sound local decision making. The creation of the Euro, their common currency, probably laid the very foundation of the ills that now plague some major European countries. A currency must reflect the economic power and work ethics of a nation, and efficient Germany sharing the same currency with a more wasteful Greece, is a bureaucratic lunacy. After Germany's Deutsche Mark became the third strongest currency in the world together with the Dollar and the Swiss Franc, some European politicians decided to reign in the power of Germany, and the result was a cumbersome, expensive, bureaucratic union with a common, artificial currency that does not reflect a clearly defined economic base.

The havoc this decision wrought with Italy, my favorite vacationing country, is a prime example of this centralized folly. When growing up in the forties, the experts told us that Italy was a poor country, close to bankruptcy. Yet, when I visited this magnificent state the first time in 1949, I was impressed by the diligence and happy attitude of its people. They were friendly and welcomed tourists with open arms, and had started to export wine, fruit, furniture, colorful designs, sausages, cheese, and other typical Italian goods.

The country started to flourish, and in the North, cities like Turin and Milan were bustling with economic activity. The less developed South received billions in funds through the government program "Il Sviluppo de Mezzogiorno." To keep exports at low prices and to fight inflation, the government regularly devalued its currency, the Lira.

This had little adverse effect for the population which simply received higher denominated salaries. Exports kept booming and tourism skyrocketed. The government issued bonds to finance its activities and rich Italians bought the government papers and got richer collecting the good dividends and investing even more. Tax evasion became a national pastime forcing the central government to reign in their wasteful spending. At the same time, an underground economy started to grow dramatically and by some estimates exceeded thirty percent. The central government had no other chance but to introduce a high sales tax, above twenty percent, to collect the necessary revenue. The low tax morale reflected the disapproval of the average Italian with the corruption and political infighting in Rome. Recent elections further document this deep aversion to the antics of politicians.

This all changed with the introduction of the artificial currency, the Euro, touted by the predominantly socialist governments in Europe as the solution to solve most financial ills of major member states as a result of their excessive spending.

International bankers then started to evaluate the Italian economy, accepting government statistics and ignoring the power of the shadow economy. They declared Italy a financial risk and interest rates on government bonds increased dramatically. These were the same bankers that flogged mortgage backed securities with a triple A rating! They also forgot that most government statistics lack credibility.

Think of Churchill's comment: "The only statistics you can trust are those you falsified yourself." The article in the respected publication, *The Economist*, headlined: "which inflation would you like, please." It explained in details the false assumptions governments make when collecting and using data. Most pundits in America talk about the high unemployment citing a figure of close on eight percent, a totally irrelevant statistic. There are close to twelve million hard working, God fearing Mexicans that do the work that Americans don't want to perform. They are not included in these published statistics.

Italian tourism and exports started to suffer from the high prices inflicted by the common currency, the Euro. The same, of course, is true with Spain and other weaker nations in the Union. Now, Germany again calls the shots to the great annoyance of some other member states, while at the same time, the German people are getting tired of supporting the weaker countries.

In retrospect, the forced centralization and the creation of a dream currency by out-of-touch bureaucrats is creating havoc within this mammoth political and economic union. Many American pundits and government officials praised the success of the Euro while totally ignoring its adverse economic effects. There is no official data available but some estimate that two trillion Euros are parked in offshore assets with the Germans alone holding in excess of two hundred billion in untaxed funds. In addition, it is estimated that around twenty percent of the German economy is underground. When I traveled thru a German region where unemployment was over twenty percent, I didn't see any men on the streets. My host, a regional banker, explained that everybody was working underground, with the tradesmen bartering their service with other unemployed workers.

Americans should learn from the dangers of centralization and return again more power to the individual states. If the Federal Government makes a mistake, the whole nation suffers, whereas if one state goes in the wrong direction, the other states may benefit.

The 2012 U.S. election was a classic case of candidate mishandling by their advisors. Either these so-called experts have never studied history or were totally immersed in the Washington Tower of Babel. The first simple rule if you want to win is: "United we win."

These publicity hungry advisory fools threw their Republican candidates to the wolves where they attacked each other for months on prime television. They would have done well to listen more to the brilliant analytical mind and formidable strategist Charles Krauthammer. The only wise candidate was Gingrich, who warned at the outset not to attack each other, but to lay out their plans and criticize the opposition. When he gained in the polls, the Romney campaign launched a vicious personal attack, spending millions which reflected poorly on his judgment and revealed a cold personality, the fastest way to loose the women vote. Reagan's "Eleventh Commandment" seems appropriate: "Thou shall not talk ill of a fellow Republican." Not one candidate had the courage to favorably mention the Bush years.

This spectacle was a disgrace, a total waste of money, and many supporters tightened their purse strings in disgust and stayed home rather than vote. Some of my acquaintances from Massachusetts, both Democrats and Republicans, confirmed that Romney was a stuffed shirt removed from the ordinary people. However, Americans mostly prefer street smart, down-to-earth politicians such as Clinton, Reagan with his astute "kitchen cabinet," or Harry Truman, whose public philosophy was epitomized by his statement: "The buck stops here." They didn't care all that much about intellectual candidates such as Stevenson or Dewey.

The Republicans would do well to review their tortuous way to select a candidate. They may take a closer look as to how the Vatican selects a Pope. Why don't the leaders of the Republican Party meet at a place without the presence of journalists and vote to select their presidential and vice presidential candidate, who will then be presented at the Convention. This would avoid these protracted fights among the contenders for the highest office. Instead of fanning white smoke thru a chimney; they may consider throwing a happy barbeque party after a successful vote. In this context it is well to remember that conservatives in all major countries find it more difficult to select a leader because these parties have a larger number of power seeking, successful leaders than are prominent on the left. When parties cannot settle on a male leader, they elect a strong woman such as Maggie Thatcher, Angela Merkel, Golda Meir or Julia Gillard. These are all excellent leaders talking common sense, facts rather than political double talk as in Washington today.

Another suggestion to solve this problem of a public attack spectacle is for the Republican presidential candidates to spend their money on opposition attack ads and lay out before the public their own ideas how to solve major problems such as Obamacare, Medicaire and Social Security, the main budget busters. The presidential candidate could then be chosen at the Convention, after the candidates' ads have appeared in all major media, educating the public about the difference between Democrats and Republicans, while at the same time countering the heavy spending by Unions.

Unfortunately many women vote for handsome, young candidates which can be risky. It was John F.

Kennedy who almost started the Third World War during the Cuban Missile Crisis. If the Russian generals hadn't called back Krushev, a global disaster may have occurred. Instead, all the Russian Prime Minister could do is take off his shoe at the United Nations and bang the table. Young men are often impetuous and shoot from the hip. Older men tend to be wiser and more restrained and thus are more likely to avoid wars. Many societies have elder councils to take advantage of the advice of older men.

One can only hope that Marco Rubio doesn't get mishandled as Romney was, but that he stays steadfast to his true character rather than becoming another Washington clone. If Hillary Clinton runs, he wouldn't stand a chance as a Romney-like apparatchik; after all she is the most admired politician according to some surveys.

Not one of the 2012 Republican candidates was willing to stop the viral attacks and concentrate on Obama's credibility gap. Throughout his campaign, Obama constantly emphasized that he had inherited the recession from the previous administration. This claim was the most effective political untruth and remained unchallenged by the Republicans. As the Republican Presidential Candidate, Romney not once pointed out that this claim was totally false. The Bush administration did not push mortgages for the masses. It was the active forces within the Democratic Party who touted Freddy Mac and Fanny Mae as solid lenders with some of the party's political leaders even enjoying financial benefits for their support.

The Bush Administration did not sign the law allowing Banks to speculate, it was President Clinton. The warnings by Christopher Cox, Bush's Chairman of the Securities and Exchange Commission, was conveniently ignored by Nancy Pelosi and Harry Reid.

Obama brilliantly masked the stark truth as to who was mainly responsible for the recession. It was in fact the American public with the help of the government and the banks. It was home buyers that took on too much debt; couples that applied for an additional mortgage when their property rose in value; individuals that maxed out their credit cards; and stock market gamblers who took out credit on their paper profits. This euphoria could not possibly last and to primarily blame Congress or the Bush Administration for the recession is blatantly wrong.

One thing is absolutely clear; Obama is without doubt an excellent President, not for the U.S., but for the Democratic Party. He is incessantly campaigning, vilifying and blaming the Republicans for all the Nation's ills. It is more and more becoming a broken recording and it will eventually be recognized as poor national leadership. He should rise to the occasion and become a bipartisan President of the entire U.S. If he continues with his present partisan stance, he will go down in history as nothing more than a narcissistic demagogue who accomplished little except burdening the Nation with more and more regulations, a bureaucratic, expensive and inefficient monstrosity, centralized healthcare, and having supported the inefficient with his financial stimulus.

I was lucky, I started to admire America as a boy; fell in love with this great nation as a soldier; and gained respect for its people that took advantage of all the opportunities available. Unfortunately, Obama grew up in an atmosphere of vilification and open hatred of the ruling establishment as exemplified by the Reverend Jeremiah Wright, who spewed hatred in the Church attended by Obama for many years.

Obama's political acumen was strengthened by Chicago's, politically correct, gutter politics. His administration is now revealed to persecute Republicans with the powerful weapon of the IRS, and accusing critical journalists of serious crimes. The Republicans had a similar leader whose staff accused and persecuted any and all that didn't agree with their politics. Leading Hollywood stars and top directors and producers were blacklisted and lost their job. They despised left leaning citizens and denounced them as communists. Luckily, their leader was only a Senator, Joseph McCarthy.

At the peak of my company's success, we were a large advertising client of *Forbes Magazine*, and I had the pleasure of having lunch with Steve Forbes when he visited Germany. I have never met a more brilliant economist. He outshone such politically motivated experts as the Nobel Price winner Paul Krugman. In this context, *The Economist* magazine's observation is worth remembering: "Garbage collectors understand more about the state of the economy than many economists. A drop in the luxury garbage signals a slowing economy."

Steve's comment: "A blowout of spending by the federal government, its overregulation of business and confusing tax code are some of the barriers that are thwarting economic recovery," is aptly summing up today's major problems. Governments should finance themselves, in addition to low taxation, by issuing treasury bonds. It is a much better way, for the State must pay interest to the bond buyers and this demands more discipline in spending rather than tax, tax, and spend.

To blame Obama for the lack of job creation is just as economically unsound as lauding Clinton for the budget surplus. The U.S. economy is like a gigantic tanker, it takes time for measures to have effect. George H. W. Bush, the forty-first President, got into a recession at the end of his term, but already in his last quarter the economy started to bounce back with the resulting revenue boost during the Clinton years. Obama should create a positive economic climate rather than play politics with so called financial cliffs which bring on doubt and uncertainty about the future, thus impeding job growth. To continue to blame the Republicans may be welcome fodder for his base, but it is poison for the economy.

The argument of the ultra left that trickle down economics doesn't work reveals their difficulties to face reality. Suppose you have one million rich Americans and ten million poor, it is quite obvious who moves the economy. The rich and well-off buy large houses, need tradesmen, buy expensive cars, enjoy luxury goods and spend vast amounts of money, while paying the bulk of the income tax. It isn't trickle down economics, it is moving up economics!

High taxes', soaking the rich, hasn't worked in any country. High taxes destroy jobs or may only create more government employment. The British suffered from the brain drain as a result of high taxes. At the same time, the Swedes were confronted with a massive outflow of capital with purchases of properties in Spain with untaxed funds, and the wide spread use of flourishing tax heavens. The tax authorities had to investigate in Spain who bought these properties and confront their citizens in Sweden.

During the Eisenhower Presidency, the top tax rate was over ninety percent for anyone with an income of more than four hundred dollars a year. The result was again an exodus of many top earners, especially stars and producers, which turned Hollywood into a desert with movies being filmed abroad.

Germany, France and Italy have also suffered as a result of high taxation with the surrounding tax heavens, Luxembourg, Switzerland and Liechtenstein benefiting greatly from these mistaken policies. A fair tax, such as a flat tax, makes more sense than progressive taxation which denies the equality guaranteed by the U.S. Constitution.

What surprised me a great deal, when I first came to America was that you could buy goods without immediate payment. In Switzerland, we had to save up for a major purchase, often waiting months before being able to enjoy it. I much prefer the American system, "Buy now. Pay later." At the same time, I am aware of the inherent dangers to take on too much debt. Of course, enjoying the goods and paying later with an inflation reduced value of the currency isn't a bad deal for the consumer.

Many experts, especially those working for banks or governments, encourage people to save, probably the most wasteful form of accumulating or preserving wealth. The measly savings rate in most industrialized nations doesn't even cover the lowest inflation rate, but banks and the government gain from this supposedly healthy investment behavior. It is better to buy precious metals, higher yielding bonds or blue chips that pay a decent dividend. Common sense dictates to mostly ignore bank or government advice as it is usually formulated in their own best interest.

Conservative candidates in the U. S. find it more and more difficult to gain sufficient support with so many citizens relying on government entitlements. These citizens view the big money pot in Washington as a bottomless source for well-being, forgetting that this never satisfied mantra has to be fed with the hard earned cash of the working population. The center right had it easier when theoretically there were three parties rather than only two as today.

The breakaway faction of the Democratic Party, the Dixicrats, formed in 1948, opposed Harry Truman.

Later to protect the Southern way of life, the Bowl weevils, conservative Southern Democrats, voted in favor of tax cuts, increase in military spending and deregulation that Reagan favored. Some of these conservative leaders like Sam Rayburn, Storm Thurmond and Harry Bird were more to the right than many Republicans. In the early 1990's we had the democratic "Blue Dogs" espousing conservative, pro-business views. Unfortunately, today all we have is the left, driven by envy, and the right, driven by greed, and these two extremes are mostly incapable to agree on compromise in the best interest of the country. All they are engaging in is blaming each other with the President being in the forefront of this destructive gamesmanship.

Billions are being spent on crime prevention, talks of gun control and government intrusion, but the root causes are being neglected. The police that are responsible for our security are so badly paid that many are tempted to augment their income by other means. Corruption is wide spread and the professional standards have been lowered. Society is willing to pay millions to a football star while paying peanuts to the valiant policemen that risk their lives every single day. Elaborate funerals and fund raisers for the bereaved family are a sad testimony to the blind attitude of the people and their representatives. In addition press reports of policemen having to shoot a criminal, often get criticized by the left wing press, while the victim receives positive coverage. Policemen, Nurses and Teachers deserve higher pay; they are the very pillars of a healthy society.

Americans should stop fighting wars. Our leaders are no longer capable of conducting efficient wars by eradicating the enemy as done in the Second World War. What is the purpose in our soldiers getting killed, loosing limbs and their health for little or no gain in countries that are totally irrelevant to our safety? Let us destroy the enemy when he is visible or when he plans attacks from within. Cut all Foreign Aid. It only corrupts and lowers the respect of the recipients. We could employ our soldiers and use the saved money more efficiently at home. Obviously, the politicians have not learned much from history. You do not negotiate with dictators, and sanctions accomplish little since there will always be nations that break ranks and supply these crooks.

The U.S. State Department, in earlier times referred to as "Foggy Bottom," hasn't learned much from history either. They plotted and helped to overthrow potentates and dictators friendly to the U.S. such as the Shah of Persia, Battista and Mubarak, only to get fanatic clerics, a communist leader and the Muslim Brotherhood. All in the mistaken belief that America's "Democratic Way of Life" can be exported to any and all nations.

To gain respect, the U.S. must threaten to use force to stop this little Caesar in North Korea from developing nuclear arms and produce long distance rockets to deliver these weapons of mass destruction. The same applies to Iran. Negotiations have achieved nothing except giving these corrupt leaders more time to develop nuclear weapons. It is now time to call their bluff and destroy their main centers, if they do not desist and allow total inspection of all facilities.

Instead of fighting useless ground wars in countries of little or no importance to the U.S., such as Afghanistan, where brave soldiers loose their lives, or limbs and mental health, let us build military compounds along the border with all the amenities, and have all the illegal immigrants come to a check point where they will be issued a rifle and uniform after a thorough health check. Impose the requirement that they serve honorably in the Armed Forces and will become Americans when they receive an honorable discharge and learn English. After all, that is what was expected of me when I immigrated to the U.S.

The money saved from cutting Foreign Aid could also be used to build closed compounds outside of big cities to help drug addicts, providing them with excellent medical care. These compounds should not be jail-like but rather provide comfortable amenities with movies, swimming pools and other facilities. After all, we spend money on this type of facilities for terrorists, rather than executing them.

The Germans were more efficient in the 1970's. They were faced with domestic terrorism by a violent leftist group calling itself the Red Army Faction, The Baader-Meinhof Gang which was dedicated to the violent overthrow of the capitalist society. Some ultra left journalists even sympathized with their aim. However, the gang's indiscriminate bombings and random killings convinced everybody that it was necessary to take drastic action. Their leader Andreas Baader was finally shot in front of my garage at Hofeckweg 2 in Frankfurt. The Germans built an expensive, high security complex where they incarcerated the rest of the gang. Conveniently, a few months later, all got poisoned in the prison with the State having saved a great deal of money.

I wish Americans would consider more severe actions with terrorists, drug dealers, rapists and other violent criminals rather than coddling them in prisons for the rest of their lives at great expense to society. Prisons are the academies of crime; and corruption and killings are widespread in them. Those that oppose executions on religious grounds must be respected, but these noble believers must bow to the majority that isn't in favor of keeping these criminals in jail for life. It doesn't make economic nor humane sense. A drug dealer that ruins many human lives should be shot on sight if two policemen see him engaged in selling drugs. Jury trials are too expensive and can be tampered with. The military has always executed deserters and society should rid itself of destroyers of human life as well.

Noble socialist ideas can have dangerously devastating effects on society, because many human beings are anything but noble. A typical example is child support for the unmarried and needy. The basic idea is very civil but the end result can be exceedingly bad. If unwed mothers have children with the sole aim to collect government financial support, these children, mostly without a father, have less chance to succeed later in life with their mothers being driven by greed, rather than love. The state should help once and then demand sterilization before helping one more time.

The riots and recent election results in the various member states of the European Union, The EU, clearly demonstrate that once citizens are accustomed to government help, it is difficult to wean them off these handouts. In National Parks signs warn visitors not to feed the animals, because eventually they cannot feed themselves. Human nature is not much different. It is imperative that governments cease to provide almost unlimited benefits without making the public aware of the ensuing costs. A retired doctor working for the Social Security Administration to screen citizens on

Social Security Disability estimated that the number could be reduced by around fifty percent if enough staff were available to investigate the legitimacy of cases.

The U.S. member states should start to force the Federal Government to properly account for its expenditures with a detailed annual budget, and if need be, the Governors of three quarters of the states should try to change the Constitution with an amendment to let the states collect the income tax and negotiate yearly with the Federal Government what it needs to fulfill its obligations.

This way each state's citizens could be made aware of how much money is available to take care of their administration and what percentage has to be paid to the Federal Government. This would remove the power of Washington to bribe voters with benefits on a federal level and return the responsibility to more easily controllable state administrations. The idea of a bottomless money pot in Washington would rapidly evaporate. After all, the Constitution has already been amended twenty seven times and now it is more important than ever to reverse the trend of centralization. To take away the power to tax is the best way to proceed. There are two organizations that cannot handle money; centralized governments because they steal it and banks because they get it mostly with false promises.

Voters should try to elect at least one candidate in each state that promises to introduce a term limit for members of Congress. With close to seventy percent of Americans being in favor of such a move, perhaps the politicians may be forced to vote on such a bill which would bring fresh blood to Washington. Everything is possible in these United States!

The fact that the present trend of more and more centralization is definitely dangerous should be clear to most Americans. Local problem solving is the better way. States would compete with each other for a healthy business climate, lower taxes and sound budgeting which would immensely strengthen the entire Union. No more federal bailouts; let local communities decide on these matters.

Emperors of the Roman Empire tried to bribe their population with bread and circus, but in the end, they lost. Don't let the Little Caesars continue to do the same in Washington.

The last thing American politicians should do is look to The European Union, EU, for good ideas, for this centralized behemoth is literally starting to fall apart. Italy, Spain, Greece and some other nations are thinking seriously about opting out of the Euro. Eventually, they have no other choice than to take care of their own destiny, rather than relying on incompetent bureaucrats in Brussels.

Journalists, pundits and TV personalities should start to recognize that purely politically motivated news reporting either on the left or on the right is detrimental to further healthy debate with the aim of achieving much needed compromise. Their intolerant actions accomplish nothing more than giving exposure to known politicians that revel in repeating their political credo over and over again. With the main public watching the programs and reading the articles that support their views, little can be changed for the better since their opinions are consistently supported without giving the other side a chance to present their case fairly.

Luckily, there are some news makers that are more professional and avoid blatant political drivel. Bob Woodward, Ron Williams, John Stewart, Anderson Cooper, Dana Perino and Bill O'Reilly as well as Bernie Goldberg come to mind. As a press secretary Jay Carney is doing an excellent job, answering often difficult questions with an engaging, enigmatic smile. The mouthpieces of the ultra left and ultra right don't deserve mentioning, because they are threatening to a fair democratic process. They promulgate hatred and intolerance such as comparing Senator John McCain to Senator Joe McCarthy. This isn't journalism; it is pandering to the lowest instincts of fanatics, a dangerous trend, undermining the very moral fabric that makes America a great nation.

Finally, it should become apparent to any thinking American that statistics supporting political arguments are largely unreliable. As a typical example, the cost of the Iraq war was negatively reported as above three trillion, while some pundits quoted it at one trillion. Both sides forgot to mention that most of these funds were spent in the U.S building planes, helicopters, humvees, tanks, rockets and supplying other war material, all of which greatly contributed to the growth of the U.S. economy. The winding down of the war obviously had the opposite effect. In comparison, the Obama stimulus packet came close to one trillion only.

The discussion about the deficit is often equally colored by political credo. The question is the relationship of the deficit as a proportion of the Gross Domestic Product, GDP, and on what the money was being spent. If the bulk went to build infrastructure and increase efficiency in productivity, it is an excellent investment and the word deficit is decidedly misleading. To compare the U.S. with Greece, as some pundits do, is downright ludicrous.

Research conducted by James K. Glassman, published in *Forbes Magazine* sheds some light on the performance of the last five Presidents in relationship to their spending and deficits. Ronald Reagan's average was 4.2%, deficit to GDP; George H. Bush's average was also 4.2%; Bill Clinton's average was 0.5%; George W. Bush's average was 2.7% and Barack Obama's so far 9.9%.

When it comes to spending, according to the source, *"The Economic Report of the President"* reveals the following: George W. Bush spent 19.6% of GDP; Clinton 19.8%; Reagan over 21%; and Obama 24.1% so far the highest level since The Second World War.

The scare mongering about the Trade Deficit is equally misleading. It is a historic fact as Frederic Bastiat, the liberal theorist and economist rightly pointed out already in the eighteenth century, that successful and growing economies have larger trade deficits than shrinking economies. Obviously, Americans prefer to buy a television made in China for a thousand dollars than paying four thousand dollars for the same product made in the U.S. China gets paid in dollars and the U.S. is richer by one television. The so called Trade Deficit reflects the power of a nation to import goods which can bring great benefits to its consumers.

The accompanying argument that the U.S. is deeply in debt to China is equally irrelevant. The Chinese accumulate dollars and the U.S. benefits from the imported goods. The Chinese are forced to invest their dollars in treasury bonds and other dollar assets, and if they decide to dump these investments, they simply get more dollars. The statement that the seller is more powerful than the buyer is simply wrong. When the U.S. reduced its imports from Japan, their economy took a decisive hit. It is the importer who decides where to buy the goods he wants.

If the American political powers start supporting drilling for Oil in the U.S. the nation will become energy independent and the potentates in the Middle East will loose billions of dollars the U.S. spends on oil imports. In addition, these mostly corrupt leaders would have fewer funds available supporting their Muslim terrorists.

The power of the U.S. economy is second to none, and to belittle America's achievements is the futile pastime of misled pessimists.